T0155148

JESUS CHRIST SUPERSTITION

JESUS CHRIST SUPERSTITION

Robert M. Price

Pitchstone Publishing
Durham, North Carolina

Pitchstone Publishing
Durham, North Carolina
www.pitchstonepublishing.com

Copyright © 2019 Robert M. Price

All rights reserved.
Printed in the USA

10 9 8 7 6 5 4 3 2 1

Library of Congress Cataloging-in-Publication Data

Names: Price, Robert M., 1954- author.
Title: Jesus Christ superstition / Robert M. Price.
Description: Durham, North Carolina : Pitchstone Publishing, 2019. |
    Includes bibliographical references.
Identifiers: LCCN 2019016900 (print) | ISBN 9781634311908 (pbk. : alk.
    paper)
Subjects: LCSH: Jesus Christ--Person and offices--Miscellanea. | Common
    fallacies--Miscellanea. | Superstition.
Classification: LCC BT203 .P745 2019 (print) | LCC BT203 (ebook) |
DDC
    232--dc23
LC record available at https://lccn.loc.gov/2019016900
LC ebook record available at https://lccn.loc.gov/2019980952

For John Loftus, a living refutation of the gospel proverb,
"The disciple is not greater than his master."

Contents

Introduction   9

1. What an Imaginary Friend We Have in Jesus   17

2. You Believe in Things You Don't Understand   47

3. My God Is Fear   79

4. The Neurosis Testament   93

5. Charis-magic   105

6. Devil's Advocates   117

7. Divination   127

8. The Retreat from Radical Prayer   157

   Conclusion: Superstitionatural   187

   About the Author

Introduction

Just what is "superstition"? It is related to *phobias*, which are unreasonable fears, fears that are not justified by any impending threat or danger. A superstition, too, usually involves groundless fears. The superstitious person has certain beliefs, inherited from popular culture and family tradition, that certain actions will produce destructive results without any real-world causal connection. Why should walking under an open ladder curse one with bad luck? Obviously, carelessly stepping under the ladder might topple a can of paint resting on the top. But that is not what the superstitious person fears. He or she dreads some ill fortune not directly brought about by any natural connection. Why would a black cat crossing one's path make one a lightning rod for misfortune? Or opening an umbrella inside your house? Or breaking a mirror? Spilling salt? And so on. Conversely, why should rubbing a rabbit's foot, clutching a four leaf clover, throwing a pinch of salt over one's shoulder, avert such disaster?

If someone believes these things, what is the nature of such beliefs? They must be distinguished from other pre- or non-scientific beliefs such as demon possession, where one's illness or mania is supposed to be the result of invasion by an evil disembodied entity. In an extended sense, the belief in possession might be considered superstition, though, unlike the black cat business, there would at least be a supposed causal connection, as in L. Ron Hubbard's classic tale "Fear" wherein a couple of loitering devils overhear a man scoffing at belief in demons and decide to show him how wrong he is. I should consider belief in possession an example of ancient science, akin to alchemy and astrology, even belief that the rainbow is Jehovah's war bow hanging in the sky. All these notions are products of intellectual ingenuity, only unaided by scientific technology.

But the same cannot be said for a belief in unlucky cats and ladders. These connections are altogether arbitrary. As far as I know, no superstitious person has tried to explain how and why the deeds in question produce the bad results. If you could find out *why* the black cat brings bad luck, maybe you could prevent it. But why bother? Isn't it simpler just to jump out of the cat's way? Just to steer clear of ladders?

The title of the present book suggests a connection between superstition and religion, specifically Christianity. I think of Plutarch's statement: "The atheist believes there is no God; the superstitious man believes there is a God but wishes there weren't." Once I spoke with a woman who was hag-ridden by the belief that God hated her and was sending all sorts of misfortune her way, to punish her for not worshipping him. Plutarch might as well have been talking about this woman, Janine. I have never met anyone like her. She was not religious, or would not have thought of herself as such, but was not hers a religious belief? There is most definitely a God, a spiteful and vindictive one, who is firing bullets with Janine's name on them! She was much like Job in the Bible, unfairly plagued by Jehovah, though he knew he had done nothing to deserve such treatment. Job was pretty indignant, but he didn't go so far as to hate God.

Neither did any of the biblical writers. They blamed themselves, or rather Israel as a whole, for their troubles: military defeats, exiles, pestilences, famines, etc. The Deuteronomic theology (so called because we find it set forth in the Book of Deuteronomy) held that God had made a covenant agreement with Israel. Henceforth he should be their God and they should be his faithful people. As long as they worshipped Jehovah (Yahweh) alone, forswearing other deities and all idols, God would watch over them, protecting them from their enemies, from disease, from famine, etc. But if his people transgressed the terms of the deal, they could not expect their divine patron to hold up his end of the bargain. The way the Old Testament writers told it, the numerous catastrophes that overtook Israel/Judah were the result of Israel's faithlessness. This self-abnegating conclusion was entirely deductive. The Bible writers thought the same way Job's blame-laying companions did: if misfortune strikes you down, you *must* have deserved it. The Deuteronomic "historians" (authors of Joshua, Judges, Samuel, and Kings) often fabricated sins to justify the disasters. Why? Because the alternative would be even worse: admitting that there was no covenant, and no God, at least no justice. This would mean man is alone in an indifferent universe with no protection and no reason to hope that the right, and the righteous, will prevail.

I would have to call this belief "superstitious" for the simple reason that the supposed cause behind misfortunes is an after-the-fact rationalization based on *ad hoc* unseen factors rather than observation. Causation that is posited to rescue religious belief seems to me little different from positing inexplicable connections between a sauntering feline and bad luck. And, just so as not to discriminate, I would say the same thing about the Hindu-Buddhist-Jainist belief in Karma, where a "good" reason for any tragedy or affliction may be dreamed up in order to protect the belief in cosmic justice. "Master, who sinned, this man or his parents, that he was born blind?" (John 9:2).

Another major feature of orthodox, traditional Christianity as superstition concerns *biblical literalism*, the stubborn insistence that all the narrated miracles really happened in the same history we live in, that the world was created inside of a week, that dinosaurs and humans lived side by side, that there is a personal devil, etc. These beliefs were not always superstitions. No one knew any better in biblical times. But since the advent of science and historical methodology, believing these things is a very different proposition. As Paul Tillich[1] explains it, it is a question of *natural* (or naïve) versus *reactive* (or reactionary) literalism. Fundamentalists in the modern world know they are defying and opposing a consensus. Their ancestors were *part* of the pre-scientific consensus. But today's literalists know they are swimming against the stream. And they will resort to contrived pseudo-science to try to salve their intellectual conscience, even though their efforts at apologetics are only more embarrassing. I used to do this sort of thing with my daughters when they were little: I would try to "explain" how Santa Claus made it down all the chimneys in a single night. But I knew I was telling white lies. I don't think biblical inerrantists,

---

1. Paul Tillich, *Dynamics of Faith*. World Perspectives Series. Harper Torchbooks (NY: Harper & Row, 1958), pp. 51–53.

"Scientific Creationists," etc., are consciously lying. They should know better, but they don't. They won't *let* themselves know better. Their literalism, as a mental operation, is the same as believing in superstitions.

> Those who live in an unbroken mythological world feel safe and certain. They resist, often fanatically, any attempt to introduce an element of uncertainty by "breaking the myth," namely, by making conscious its symbolic character. Such resistance is supported by authoritarian systems, religious or political, in order to give security to the people under their control and unchallenged power to those who exercise the control.[2]

But we don't want to miss the trees for the forest. Does the Bible not only take for granted a prescientific world view but also depict, without embarrassment, particular superstitious practices? In fact it does. In Genesis 35:25–31:16 Jacob selectively breeds goats marked with stripes and spots by having some of Laban's herd mate in front of wooden stakes from which he has peeled away strips of bark. This is a plain case of imitative magic, in short, superstition. Nothing is said of it being the result of a special divine intervention. It is simply stated without any implication that anything extraordinary is going on.

When the Philistines suspected that Jehovah had smitten them with the Black Plague, their shamans suggested an experiment: load the stolen Ark of the Covenant on the bed of an ox cart and let the oxen carry it wherever they will. If they make a bee-line for the Israelite border, that will confirm

---

2. Tillich, *Dynamics of Faith,* p. 51.

that Jehovah was the culprit and wanted his Ark back (1 Sam. 5:6–12; 6:1–12). The premise was that if one creates a zone of randomness, one has opened a window through which God may act. The apostles thought the same way in Acts 1:11–26, when they narrowed down candidates to replace Judas Iscariot to two men. Basically, they flipped a coin or drew straws. They cast lots, regarding the outcome not as random luck but rather as the will of God. Something similar occurs at the Last Supper when Jesus clandestinely designates the one who is about to turn him over to the authorities: "Whoever dips with me into the dish." It turns out, of course, to be the Iscariot. There are twelve men present, all of them at one moment or another ready to dip a piece of bread into the herb sauce. Naturally speaking, it might be any of them who happens to do so at the same moment Jesus does. That is already superstition, but it seems possible that underlying the canonical version is an earlier one in which Jesus is actually *choosing* one disciple to hand him over, a necessary role that someone has to play to advance the plan of salvation. On this reading, Jesus himself does not know who will play that role but is now allowing Divine Providence to make itself known. Any way you cut it, that's what you call superstition.

Next to the sale of indulgences, the aspect of Medieval Catholicism that has attracted the most scathing ridicule from Protestants is the veneration of relics. These have included shavings from the True Cross, bones of the apostles, holy shrouds, even milk from the Virgin Mary and feathers from the Holy Ghost! Holy relics are neither mere museum pieces nor souvenirs. Rather, they are believed to be imbued with some of the sacred power or sanctity of the former possessors of these objects. In other words, it is contagious (contiguous) magic.

Surely such rank superstition cannot be found in scripture? Think again! What do you think is going on in 2 Kings 13:21 when, in the face of sudden danger, some men on burial detail toss a corpse into the open mausoleum of Elisha where the prophet's corpse must have been laid out for permanent viewing (like Lenin's tomb!). The corpse lands on the remains of the prophet and springs back to life! That's one heck of a relic!

Jesus is still alive while a fan benefits from his relic, namely his prayer shawl, in Mark 5:24–34. "If I can just touch the hem of his garment . . .!" And sure enough, "power goes out from him." Even more bizarre, Acts 19:12 tells us that people unable to get an appointment with the Apostle Paul nonetheless managed to grab his handkerchiefs and work aprons in hopes enough of his miracle-working *mojo* still clung to them to heal whomever one placed them on. And it worked![3]

How about Necromancy? Trafficking with the dead? King Saul banned the practice (1 Sam. 28:1–25) but later resorted to it. Isaiah 8:19 condemns the practice: "When someone tells you to consult mediums and spiritists, who whisper and mutter, should not a people inquire of their God? Why consult the dead on behalf of the living?" (NIV). But it is pretty clear that the biblical writers did not deny the reality of spiritualism or mediumism. No, it was a question of authorized versus unauthorized methods of augury. The Bible writers represent the priestly establishment who tried to control access to revelation, restricting it to the Urim and Thummim (a kind of oracular dice), the ephod (a breastplate vestment encrusted with twelve gems, ostensibly standing for the twelve tribes

---

3. This reminds me of how Elvis's adoring fans used to tear off bits of his clothing. Once he kissed my cousin Cathy, and she wouldn't wash that cheek for days!

but probably originally representing the Zodiac), and a staff of court prophets. They wanted to silence rival voices of supernatural guidance as a means to control the populace. (Obviously this is also the motive for defining a canon of scripture: you don't want people thinking they can get guidance from the Gospel of Philip!) But Genesis presents the other side of the controversy. All those notes about the burial places of the Matriarchs, e.g., Deborah's in 35:8, must be vestiges of the use of these as pilgrimage sites to which the pious journeyed, paying priestesses to consult the ghosts of the Matriarchs to tell their fortunes. If you have ever heard fundamentalist apologists trying to explain these things away, as if the Witch of Endor had only pretended to be invoking the shade of Samuel while actually summoning a demon in disguise, you were only hearing the propaganda line of the ancient priestly authorities.

* * *

In this book my goal is to analyze certain important aspects of Christian belief that I consider superstitious in character. Often these neurotic and destructive features are unfortunate accretions to the faith and by no means essential to it. They could in principle be purged from Christianity to the glad benefit of Christians. But there are other aspects and implications of Christian belief that invite damaging critiques of Christian theology, requiring major surgery if indeed the patient is salvageable at all. I do not draw attention to the difficulties besetting Christianity with glee. I love and honor the Christian tradition, but that does not allow me to cover the sometimes unpleasant truth about it. Sometimes it is necessary to critique a thing in order to understand it.

Chapter One

What an Imaginary Friend
We Have in Jesus

You may know me as a proponent of the Christ Myth theory, the hypothesis that there was never a historical Jesus. But for our purposes here, Mythicism is neither here nor there. Go on thinking there was a historical Jesus, as indeed there may have been for all I know. So I am not suggesting that the belief in a historical Jesus qualifies as superstition. In fact, as we will soon see, the belief in a historical Jesus is threatened by what one might call the quest for the devotional Jesus.

What is the criterion for salvation? If you ask evangelical, fundamentalist, Pentecostal, and Charismatic believers, it always comes down, not to the Nicene Creed or the Westminster Confession, not to sacramental spirituality, but to cultivating a "personal relationship with Jesus Christ as personal Lord and Savior." As a student of historical, systematic, and biblical theology, I find this fact astonishing.

It strikes me as comparable to the "Jesus Only" Pentecostal sect's insistence that one must speak in tongues if one is to be "saved." A particular approach to Protestant devotionalism has been elevated to the position of the very essence of Christianity. All sorts of things are wrong with this. I propose to examine, first, the question of whether there is any scriptural basis for "personal savior" devotionalism. Second, I want to look at the implied theological and conceptual contradictions. Third, I'll consider parallels from Eastern religions, which seem to me to cast interesting light on the "personal relationship" spirituality.

You search the Scriptures for in them
you think to find eternal life,
but they speak of me.

As far as I can tell, there is simply no basis in the New Testament for the fundamentalist-evangelical gospel of the "personal relationship with Christ"/"Jesus as personal savior."[4] This is really quite remarkable in light of the fact that, to hear its advocates tell it, such piety is the end-all and be-all of the whole Bible, whether by Old Testament prediction or by New Testament depiction. It is for this reason that fundamentalists frequently organize Bible handouts as an evangelistic outreach, as if the whole book, with its turgid Leviticuses and tedious Chronicles were likely to woo the unbeliever to Christ. Even

---

4. "Pietists deny the existence of faith in those persons in whom they miss the exact demeanour and modes of speech which they have made into a ceremonial law for themselves." Albrecht Ritschl, *The Christian Doctrine of Justification and Reconciliation*. Trans. A.B. Macaulay, A.R. Gordon, R.A. Lendrum, James Strachan, and H.R. Mackintosh (Edinburgh: T. & T. Clark, 1900), pp. 119–120.

if it's just the New Testament in a bad translation like Today's English Version or The Living Bible, I'll wager that no reader, new to the text, would ever think the book is about a "personal relationship" with the gospel hero who lambastes Pharisees and withers fig trees, much less the Pauline theological cipher to whom no personality, description, or biography is ascribed.

You may think I don't know my Bible very well. How can I ignore the classic text Revelation 3:20? "Behold, I stand at the door and knock. If anyone hears my voice and opens the door I will come in to him and dine with him, and he with me." Doesn't this passage invite the reader to "have a little talk with Jesus," as the gospel song says? Or as another chorus says, "He walks with me and he talks with me, and he tells me I am his own. And the joy we share as we tarry there, no other has ever known." You know, the soft and smarmy depiction of Jesus rapping gently on the door in William Holman Hunt's painting "The Light of the World" and Warner Sallman's "Christ at Heart's Door." Surely the most elaborate treatment of this motif is Robert Boyd Munger's InterVarsity Press booklet *My Heart, Christ's Home*, which very skillfully spins the whole thing out into a narrative of a twentieth-century man who invites Jesus to share his house. This devotional version of *The Odd Couple* soon shows Jesus' housemate to be a less than perfect host, as he comes to spend less and less time with his personal savior, who waits each morning, patiently but in vain, for his best pal to join him in the parlor for a soul-searching chat. The scenario is unwittingly comedic, as it must remind the reader, Christian or not, of uncomfortable situations in which he has been cornered into a chat with some blue-nosed, pious aunt or in-law. You can sympathize with Munger's character who finds himself avoiding time spent with the holy Son of God. But of course this is not what author Munger intended, which was an allegory of the devotional life. The character corresponds to the evangelical who knows he should "commune with Christ" daily in a "quiet time" of prayer, Bible reading, and introspection, but is too easily distracted by worldly obligations. But I think this stuff has no basis in the New Testament. So what *does* Revelation 3:20 mean?

For one thing, we might ask ourselves what such a sweet devotional nostrum is doing in the psychedelic Technicolor Apocalypse of John with its bloodbaths and multi-headed dragons? Is it really a petunia in an onion patch? No, I dare say we ought to view it as another eye-stinging onion. (And that's no criticism; I happen to love the Book of Revelation!)

The Revelation of John is, for most Bible students, by far the most confusing portion of the Bible, and this is because it is written in colorful cipher-language. This goes with the territory: this sort of code is integral to the whole apocalyptic genre. Why? In some cases, the authors may have been trying to avoid trouble with pagan authorities who would consider their work subversive if it were written in plain speech. But on the whole, the motive seems to have been to make sympathetic readers "work for it," as when Jesus urges those who hear his quizzical parables, "He who has ears to hear, let him hear" (Mark 4:9; cf. Rev. 2:7, 11, 17, 29; 3:6,13,22).

What the Book of Revelation reveals is the crash-banging *end of the world*. It is, therefore, filled with *eschatology*, the lore of the Last Things. This must be understood as the basic framework of the book. And though there is much that is not easily understood by the casual reader, this much is obvious on every page. As the seven letters introducing the work to the Seven Churches of Asia Minor make clear, the author (John the Revelator) means to warn his readers of the impending Tribulation and to exhort them to vigilance and endurance in the face of it. It is striking to observe a series of double references, whereby rewards promised to the readers foreshadow the cosmic-level events of the End. Revelation 2:7 promises readers in Ephesus a snack from the Edenic Tree of Life which later appears in 22:1–2. The faithful martyrs of Smyrna will be given the crown of life (2:10), looking forward to the resurrection of martyrs in 20:4. Those in Pergamum who overcome will be given to eat of the "hidden manna," i.e., that concealed in the Ark of the Covenant (Exod.16:32–34), which is revealed from heaven in Revelation 11:19. Those in Thyatira are promised authority over the nations (2:26–27), foreshadowing 12:5; 20:4. To those in Sardis who overcome their obstacles he promises a glorious resurrection body, symbolized by radiant white robes (3:4–5), which they will don in 6:11; 19:7–8. To the righteous Philadelphians Christ promises citizenship in the New Jerusalem (3:12), which descends from the sky in 21:3. Finally, to the Laodiceans he promises they shall share the dais with him at the Messianic Banquet (3:20–21). This is going to be crucial for grasping the point of Revelation 3:20, and it is not what you have always been told.

For New Testament scholars, the first step in making sense of a passage is to try to figure out the *Sitz-im-Leben*, or life-setting that gave rise to it. A saying may sound important but still baffling as long as we don't know what kind of situation or topic is being addressed there. It's kind of like hearing only half of a telephone conversation and trying to figure who's on the other end. As for *this* conversation, the subject is pretty easy to figure out. But who is talking to whom? Who is "John"? And who are the "angels of the seven churches" to whom, it says, the letters are addressed? As for John the Revelator, we can't assume he is supposed to be John the son of Zebedee, one of the twelve disciples. John (Yohannon; Ioannes) was too common a name for it to denote any particular individual without further qualification. But Revelation itself tells or implies a few important things about him. He was a prophet channeling oracles from the ascended Christ. He is located, at present, on the Island of Patmos in the Mediterranean. Why is he there? We usually take for granted that he had been exiled there for his gospel preaching, which would certainly make sense, but the text doesn't actually say so. Perhaps we are to understand him to be there on a missionary journey. Or maybe both: he could have arrived on Patmos to preach and got arrested for it, like Paul in the Book of Acts. But I don't think that makes any difference. Historical or not, John's exile is mentioned in order to justify his prefacing the Revelation with seven cover letters. I think that is a literary device, that all seven letters are designed to be read together as we now read them.[5] But even if it is a pose, it tells us something. It presupposes a certain picture (memory?) of the Johannine community, especially when we compare Revelation's depiction with that implied in the so-called Johannine Epistles.

Are these two New Testament writers the same person? Didn't I just say there were too many guys named "John" for the name to identify one particular individual? Yes, and it's even worse than that, since 1, 2, and 3 John are actually anonymous. The author self-identifies only as "the Elder." It was only later that scribes made an educated(?) guess about his identity.

---

5. Just like the so-called Ignatian Epistles. And see Richard I. Pervo, "Romancing an Oft-Neglected Stone: The Pastoral Epistles and the Epistolary Novel." *Journal of Higher Criticism* Vol. 1, no. 1, 1994, pp. 25–47.

Further, there is no real possibility that the Johannine Epistles were written by John of Patmos. The grammar and style are just way too different. But consider this: a close reading of both sets of letters (the three from the Elder and the seven from the Revelator) presuppose a kind of diocesan arrangement with the Elder or the Revelator in a supervisory capacity. (By the way, the word "bishop" literally means "supervisor" or "overseer.") In both cases, we see the leader staying in touch with the congregations loyal to him by means of both individual and encyclical letters carried by itinerant prophets, called "brethren" in 3 John and "angels" or "messengers" (same word in Greek, *angelos*) in Revelation. Both sets of church communities were subject to sectarian strife of a gnostic character. First John warns that some of the circuit-riding brethren had begun to propagate a docetic doctrine, i.e., Jesus was not a being of tangible flesh and blood but rather a kind of phantom (1 John 4:2–3). Others apparently taught that "Jesus was not the Christ" (1 John 2:22), i.e., the human Jesus was merely the channeler for the Christ Spirit who spoke through him up until the crucifixion. The Elder brands these "heretics" as the fulfillment of the prophecies of the Antichrist. Similarly, the seven churches of Asia Minor are dealing in various ways with the teaching of the Gnostic Nicolaitans, whom the Revelator vilifies with the same fury. I think it is likely that the authors of the Johannine Epistles and the Book of Revelation were two successive leaders of the same group of churches. (Believe it or not, this is going somewhere. We are getting closer to Revelation 3:20.)

So the angels of the seven churches are the brethren of the Johannine epistles. The seven churches constitute the Johannine sphere of influence. Much has been written in recent years about such "itinerant charismatics" in the early Christian movement.[6] They appear to be "my brethren" whose vicissitudes are catalogued in the Sheep and Goats parable in Matthew 25. "Inasmuch as you did it to the least of these my brethren, you did it to me." The people who heeded their preaching are rewarded, while those who rejected the brethren and their preaching, refusing them shelter, provisions, medicine, and prison visitation (cf. Mark 6:10–11; Phil. 1:7; 2:25; 4:10–16; Phlm. vv. 10–13), have hell to pay. To assist them or to reject them is to assist or to reject Jesus who, after all, speaks through them: "Whoever hears you hears me" (Luke 10:16). As Gerd Theissen[7] suggests, the saying, "Whoever in this sinful and adulterous generation is ashamed of me and my words, of him shall the Son of Man also be ashamed when he comes with the glory of his Father and the holy angels" (Mark 8:38) was originally understood as voiced by Jesus' earthly representatives, predicting that their preaching will be vindicated one day soon when the itinerants' heavenly patron arrives to wipe the sneers off their unbelieving kissers.

Even the Eucharistic miracle in Luke 24 can be understood as referring to the wandering journeymen of the gospel.[8] On

---

6. Gerd Theissen, *Social Reality and the Earliest Christians: Theology, Ethics, and the World of the New Testament*. Trans. Margaret Kohl (Minneapolis: Fortress Press, 1992); Stevan L. Davies, *The Revolt of the Widows: The Social World of the Apocryphal Acts* (Carbondale: Southern Illinois University Press, 1980).

7. Gerd Theissen, *Sociology of Early Palestinian Christianity*. Trans. John Bowden (Philadelphia: Fortress Press, 1978), pp. 7, 27.

8. Richard J. Dillon, *From Eye-Witnesses to Ministers of the Word*. Analectica Biblica 82 (Rome: Biblical Institute Press,

Easter Sunday, two dejected disciples who, so to speak, do not yet realize it *is* Easter Sunday, are trudging back home to Emmaus when they are joined by a stranger looking for company. He tells them their disillusionment is premature. When they reach home and invite their new friend to supper, he blesses the bread and they recognize in him the risen presence of Jesus. Why do they not recognize him at first? Why only hours later, after his scripture lessons, when he consecrates the Lord's Supper? Because it *wasn't* literally Jesus. But it was one of Jesus' itinerant brethren who speak with his authoritative voice. "You received me as an angel, as Christ Jesus" (Gal. 4:14).[9] Not coincidentally, the early church manual called the *Didache* ("The Teaching of the Twelve Disciples to the Nations") says one ought to allow the travelling "apostles" considerable freedom when they conduct the Lord's Supper, as if this is the liturgical role they routinely played. The "real presence" of Christ in the Eucharist was located, not in the bread and wine, but in the celebrant. If you turned him away, if you rejected his claims to Christ's authority, you were blaspheming the Holy Spirit. And there was a close connection between the Eucharist

---

1978), pp. 239–29; John Koenig, *New Testament Hospitality: Partnership with Strangers as Promise and Mission*. Overtures to Biblical Theology no. 17 (Philadelphia: Fortress Press, 1985), p. 85–86, 91–94.

9. Hugh J. Schonfield comes surprisingly close to this understanding when he speculates the young man at the tomb in Mark, the companion of the Emmaus disciples in Luke, and the beckoning man on the shore in John 21 might have been a confederate of Jesus obeying his Lord's deathbed command for his disciples to reassemble in Galilee, but that those to whom he delivered his message mistook him for the Risen Jesus. *The Passover Plot: New Light on the History of Jesus* (NY: Bantam Books, 1967), "He Is Not Here," pp. 163–175.

and eschatology, as the earthly observance of the Supper was understood as an anticipation of the Messianic Banquet of the End Times (Rev. 19:7–9). This is why the discussion of the Lord's Supper in 1 Corinthians 11:26 and (implicitly) 16:22 concludes with the Aramaic formula *Maranatha!* "Our Lord, come!"

> But even if it is a prayer to Jesus to come to his own, the fact that it almost certainly has its context in the primitive Eucharist raises the question whether it means more than what is implied, say, in Rev. 3.20: 'Behold, I stand at the door and knock; if anyone hears my voice and opens the door, I will *come in* to him and eat with him, and he with me.'[10] (John A.T. Robinson)

Now what does all this have to do with Revelation 3:20? Well, much in every way! The verse must be taken as referring to the reception of the "angels" (messengers) of the seven churches, bearing, as they do, the letters from the Risen Christ, dictated through an angel to the Revelator. To "hear my voice" means the same thing it means in John 10:4–5, to *recognize* the voice of Jesus *as* the voice of Jesus, the real thing. Think of the eschatological scenario depicted in Matthew 7:21–23 and Luke 13:22–27. On the Day of Judgment people will be lined up at the Pearly Gates hoping to be invited to enter. But some will be awfully disappointed when Jesus, playing bouncer, tells them their names do not appear on the list. "Depart from me! I never knew you." Yikes! Jesus is on the inside and does not recognize the knockers, who come too late.

Revelation 3:20 just turns the image around: this time

---

10. John A.T. Robinson, *Jesus and his Coming* (Philadelphia: Westminster Press, 1957, 1979), pp. 26–27.

it is the glorified Jesus waiting on the doorstep until the householder must recognize *him*, and if he turns Jesus away, it is because "*I* never knew *you*." Fatal error! The guy at the door is no brush salesman, no pesky Jehovah's Witness, but a true bearer of the Word of Jesus and to be welcomed as if Jesus himself, in person. And that bearer is the messenger carrying "the Revelation of Jesus Christ which God gave him to show his servants what must soon transpire" (Rev. 1:1).

The parable of the Great Supper (Matt. 22:1–10; Luke 14:15–20) makes the same point: the host sends his servants to the dwellings of his invited guests with the news, "Supper's ready! Time to go!" But they all have better things to do. That is what Revelation 3:20 is about. And the Great Supper is the Marriage Super of the Lamb.

> We need only compare Revelation iii. 20: "*Behold, I stand at the door and knock: if any man hear My voice and open the door, I will come in to him, and will sup with him, and he with Me.*" It is the well-known eschatological notion of a Messianic supper, where all the saints will be at table with the Son of Man and the patriarchs.[11]

It has, then, not a thing to do with happy hours of a devotional quiet time wallowing in the love of Jesus. It is not necessarily incompatible with the "personal savior" business, but it certainly does not teach such a thing. And neither does any other verse of scripture. I am not saying the Bible teaches it but that it is wrong; I mean that it just isn't there to begin with. Evangelicals are foisting it on the text, one more instance of biblical ventriloquism.

---

11. Ernst von Dobschütz, *The Eschatology of the Gospels* (London: Hodder and Stoughton, 1910), p. 190–193.

Quest for the Personal Jesus

Here's an irony: in one sense it is possible that the personal savior business does have roots in the New Testament, but it doesn't exactly serve the interests of fundamentalist piety. I am thinking of Bruno Bauer's theory that there was no historical Jesus, but that the evangelist Mark created the character out of whole cloth, inspired by the words of Seneca:

> We must select some noble man whom we have always before our eyes so that we live as if he looks at what we do, and act as if he sees it. We need a guard and teacher. A great number of sins are eliminated when the stumbling person (*peccatoris*) has at his side a witness. The spirit must have somebody whom it reveres with an awe to which is added also his most secret inner being (*sanctus facit*). The mere thought of such a helper has regulating and improving power. He is a guard, an example and a norm without which one will not restore to balance whatever is wrong (Epistle 11).[12]

It is clear that Seneca was suggesting that the person concerned to perfect his character ought to pick an ego-ideal and imagine his approving or disapproving one's behavior. In modern Christian terms, this would be more like asking "What would Jesus do?" than like thinking one is "having a little talk with Jesus." And, if Christ-Mythicist Bruno Bauer was right, that's what Mark had in mind, too. But in any case, it looks

---

12. Bruno Bauer, *Christ and the Caesars: The Origin of Christianity from Romanized Greek Culture*. Trans. Frank E. Schacht (Charleston, SC: Charleston House Publishing, 1998), p. 41.

to me as if the personal savior piety did begin the same way, even if many centuries later. Consider a passage from Count Zinzendorf, the great Pietist teacher of the eighteeth century.

> When a person becomes a Christian . . . for a moment the Savior becomes present to him in person . . .I do not pretend that we see a body with our corporeal eyes . . . It is the heart that must see at least once . . . [In] reality and truth one has the Creator of all things . . . standing in his suffering form, in his penitential form, in the form of one atoning for the whole human race—this individual object stands before the vision of one's heart, before the eyes of one's inward man . . . Now this is the entrance to this state , that one receives him at this moment, looks at him longingly, and falls in love with him: that one says, "Yes, God, Creator, Holy Spirit! My eyes have seen your salvation. They have seen your little Jesus: my heart wept for joy when his nail prints, his wounds, his bloody side stood before my heart . . ."
>
> But what kind . . . of effect on our heart does his perpetual look have afterward? . . . [E]very loving look from the Savior indicates our morality to us throughout our whole life: One dissatisfied, one sorrowful, one painful look from the Savior embitters and makes loathsome to us everything that is immoral, unethical, and disorderly . . . For the only remedy against all . . . alluring demands, gross or subtle, is the doubtful glance of the Savior, when the form of Jesus does not seem so pleasing, so joyful to our hearts, when he seems to us to be no longer so sweetly before our hearts as usual. [. . .] [I]n the eyes of the tortured Lamb, there lies your blessed, happy knowledge of good and evil.[13]

13. Nicolas Ludwig, Count von Zinzendorf, *Nine Public Lectures on Important Subjects in Religion*, 1746. Trans. George W. Forell (Iowa City: University of Iowa Press). Reprinted in

Likewise, John Friedrich Starck writes in his *Daily Handbook for Days of Joy and Sorrow* (1728): "Set thy most holy presence before my eyes, that I may be the more encouraged to persevere in sanctification, and not to offend thee."[14]

It is apparent that these spiritual guides originally proposed "merely" imagining the Savior with the mind's eye to act as a personified conscience. "Gee, suppose Jesus were to spot me doing this! Yikes! Maybe I, uh, better not." Certainly not a bad idea, of course. But not yet a literal belief that one is actually chatting with the omnipresent Risen Jesus inside your head (or heart or pancreas or whatever). When it does get to that point, we are talking about an imaginary friend. What eventually happened, then, was a hardening of the original mind-game version. The same process can be observed in other religious traditions. For instance, the very ancient Samkhya system of Hinduism strove for an experience of enlightenment via meditation whereby the immortal soul freed itself of entanglement with the realm of gross matter. Samkhya was/is non-theistic. There was no role for a deity in this type of Hinduism, any more than in a diet or a system of physical exercise. Subsequently, the sage Patanjali modified Samkhya, adding to it a set of yogic disciplines absent from the original version. One feature of the new Patanjala Yoga was the addition of *Isvara* ("the Lord"), imagined as a free soul that had never been mired in matter. This *ad hoc* deity was like a man beckoning to sailors, guiding them to the farther shore of

---

Peter C. Erb, *Pietists: Selected Writings*. Classics of Western Spirituality (NY: Paulist Press, 1983), pp. 317–319.

14. John Friedrich Starck, *Daily Handbook for Days of Rejoicing and Sorrow*. Revised and reprinted from 1855 ed. In Erb, *The Pietists: Selected Writings*, p. 211.

enlightenment. "He is useful to the soul . . . rather as the ideal object of contemplation, for he is the divine exemplar of all human souls: by the contemplation of God one becomes *like* God."[15] There is reason to believe that Patanjali did not think Isvara had any objective existence. But eventually yogis began to "harden" Isvara into a real piece of theology, believing him to be a living entity.

It appears the same thing happened with the notion of a "subtle physiology" in Hatha and Tantric (Kundalini) Yogas.

> The main point of departure is that tantric *sandhya* uses the thought construct of the mystical body as conceived in the Hindu and Vajrayana Buddhist esoteric systems, i.e., the notion of the central duct surrounded by the two peripheral ducts which penetrate the *cakras* on their way to the experience of union in the higher *cakra* thought to be located beneath the cranium.
>
> All yoga discipline postulates, on the theoretical side, the existence of a secondary somatic system consisting of centres, circles, or lotuses . . . located along an imagined spinal column in that secondary body. . . . [T]his yogic body is not supposed to have any objective existence in the sense that the physical body has. It is a heuristic device aiding meditation, not any objective structure. . . . [T]he tantric texts never suggest that this body and its organs have physiological existence.[16]

---

15. R.C. Zaehner, *Hinduism* (NY: Oxford University Press, 1966), p. 71.

16. Agehananda Bharati, *The Tantric Tradition* (Garden City: Doubleday Anchor Books, 1970), pp. 247, 291.

But of course, as time went by, devotees came to believe the chakra system was quite real, and today many go so far as to suggest that the chakras are actual nerve ganglia along the spinal cord. In just the same way, I am suggesting that the notion of Jesus the personal savior began simply as a mind-game but finally hardened into the belief that "he walks with me and he talks with me, and he tells me I am his own."

But there is an even more striking parallel with Hindu and Buddhist devotion, namely *Bhakti* Yoga. This is a yoga of emotional heart-devotion to a chosen god, bodhisattva, or avatar. It is a hugely popular set of devotional cults, each centered upon one's divine favorite, whether Ram, Vishnu, Krishna, Siva, Kali, Avalokitesvara, Amida Buddha, etc. Most people simply do not have the time or the mental discipline to practice eight-stage yoga, meditation on a mantra, sitting for hours in the lotus position, fasting, sleep deprivation, etc. So what *can* they do? They can present every daily action as a sacrifice to one's savior in gratitude for the salvation he or she provides. This answers exactly to evangelical devotion to Jesus as one's personal savior. It would be fair, I think, to call evangelical piety "Jesus *bhakti.*" It is not primarily theological, like the dour cognitivism of Calvinists, but emotional.

The Knights Who Say Nee

Each pietist creates his own personal Christ from the meager evidence of gospel texts, paintings, Bible illustrations and Vacation Bible School cartoons. C.S. Lewis puts it well in *The Screwtape Letters.* The veteran demon describes a Christian at prayer:

If you examine the object to which he is attending, you will find that it is a composite object containing many . . . ingredients. There will be [e.g.] images derived from pictures of [Christ] as He appeared during . . . the Incarnation. . . . I have known cases where what the [person] called his "God" was actually located . . . inside his own head. . . . [Such a Christian will be] praying to it—to the thing that he has made, not to the Person who has made him.[17]

This, I think, is the unintended truth of the slogan of Jesus as one's "personal savior." He is a different savior in the eye of every beholder. *Your* personal savior is customized a bit differently from *mine*. He doesn't have all the same options. That is inevitable. The danger is in making Jesus a ventriloquist dummy for either your self-indulgence or your neuroses. In the former case, Jesus will go too easy on you. He will not so much have taken on himself "the form of a servant" (Phil. 2:7), as he will have become your butler, your Jeeves, your Man Friday, your servile yes-man. He will meekly do something the real Jesus would never have done, namely to rubber-stamp the whims of your own conscience. In the latter case, the imaginary Jesus of your self-hatred will speak with the voice of sacrifice and negation, calling you to the nihilistic pseudo-discipleship of withdrawing from everyone and everything you love.

Who Watches the Watchman?

Isn't it obvious that the gaze of Jesus as imagined by Zinzendorf, Munger, and the rest is really the conscience of the Christian

17. C.S. Lewis, *The Screwtape Letters and Screwtape Proposes a Toast* (NY: Macmillan, 1970), p. 22.

dressed up in costume like Jesus? I have chosen the great devotional writer Watchman Nee (Nee To-sheng) as perhaps the best proponent of this sort of self-abnegating piety, wherein Jesus speaks with the voice of the introspective pietist's own neuroses.

> If we give ourselves unreservedly to God, many adjustments may have to be made: in family, or business, or church relationships, or in the matter of our personal views. God will not let anything of ourselves remain. His finger will touch, point by point, everything that is not of him, and will say: "This must go." Are you willing? It is foolish to resist God, and always wise to submit to him.[18]

> Is there anything God is asking of you that you are withholding from him? Is there any point of contention between you and him?[19]

A man Nee calls Mr. Paul "cherished the hope from his early youth that one day he would be called 'Dr. Paul.' When he was quite a little chap he began to dream of the day when he would enter the university, and he imagined himself first studying for his M.A. degree and then for his Ph.D." He obtained his Masters, was converted, and became a preacher and church pastor, but he felt frustrated at his perceived lack of spiritual power. He prayed and fasted, asking God what was holding him back. He felt God replying, "Your heart is set on something that I do not wish you to have. You have yielded

---

18. Watchman Nee, *The Normal Christian Life* (Wheaton: Tyndale House Publishers / Fort Washington: Christian Literature Crusade, 1977), p. 105.

19. Nee, *Normal Christian Life*, p. 145.

to me all but one thing, and that one thing you are holding to yourself—your Ph.D." With only two weeks to go before his dissertation defense, he finally agreed with God to drop the whole thing, whereupon he received the full blessing of the Holy Ghost.[20]

> Our complete surrender of ourselves to the Lord generally hinges upon some one particular thing, and God waits for that one thing. He must have it, for he must have our all.[21]

Mr. Paul was like the king of Moab, besieged by Israel, who sacrificed his son in desperation, to gain the victory: "Then he took his eldest son who was to reign in his stead, and offered him for a burnt offering upon the wall. And there came great wrath upon Israel; and they withdrew from him and returned to their own land" (2 Kings 3:27). Mr. Paul assumed *something* dear to him was blocking the blessing, so his hypersensitive conscience fingered his dearest dream. At that point he *had* to sacrifice it to get the experience he craved. It was a self-fulfilling prophecy, a kind of subconscious bargain with himself.

> Many a time we have to come to the place where we are willing to let go to him things we think to be good and precious—yes, and even, it may be, the very things of God themselves—that his will may be done.[22]

---

20. Nee, *Normal Christian Life*, pp. 147–148.

21. Nee, *Normal Christian Life*, p. 148.

22. Nee, *Normal Christian Life*, p. 255.

Whatever we have as an "alabaster box": the most precious thing, the thing dearest in the world to us . . . we give that all up to the Lord.[23]

Let me tell you, dear friends, you cannot produce such impressions of God upon others without the breaking of everything, even your most precious possessions, at the feet of the Lord Jesus.[24]

Anyone who has lingered within the fundamentalist half-world knows what Nee (and the many preachers and writers whom he represents) is really saying here. He does not seem to intend the obvious, which goes without saying, namely that one must be willing to sacrifice any sinful habit or pursuit, since retaining such guilty pleasures produces ambivalence. By definition, such a one is not obeying the Great Commandment to love God with all one's heart, soul, mind, and strength. John Wesley said it well: he that is sanctified may yet discover he retains some sin, but as soon as he realizes it *is* a sin, he will not delay to repudiate it, since he loves God more than anything and automatically loathes anything displeasing to his Lord. But that is not what Nee is saying, or at least I don't think it is. As Nee eventually admits, the devoted Christian must consider anything and everything he loves or desires as a challenge to the supremacy of God in his life. Again, no one needs to be told that God must be the Christian's *ultimate concern.* If it came down to it, he must sacrifice anything incompatible with his devotion to God. But according to the Watchman, pretty much anything and everything in one's life is automatically an

---

23. Nee, *Normal Christian Life*, p. 274.

24. Nee, *Normal Christian Life*, p. 282.

idol that must be smashed. As soon as the neurotic conscience, egged on by Nee, wonders whether this hobby, that romance, the other possession might have to be sacrificed, his natural reluctance to do so is taken as the finger of God marking it as an idol. "Gee, I'd sure hate to have to give *that* up! Uh-oh! I guess that means I'd rather keep it than obey God! *Darn* it! Oh, well, another one bites the dust. . . ."

Philip Helfaer describes the hag-ridden mental state of the pietist:

> [T]he effort to do God's will is given explicit and conscious place in the context of a personal relationship with God. Every major act and decision is considered or undertaken with the question in mind, "Is this act in God's will? What is God's will in this matter?" The sense of personal relationship with God and the constant effort to do God's will may extend even to the minutiae of everyday life—to asking God the whereabouts of a mislaid pencil, for example.[25]

And how is one to determine God's will in all these matters? If there were something obviously amiss in a contemplated relationship or job offer, there would be no need to ask God's approval. Are you stupid? But this kind of Hamlet-like deliberation presupposes there is no clear argument on either side. So the whole thing is nothing but a source of continual anxiety, like a guy forever terrified of getting his bitchy girlfriend mad at him by some accidental offense.

The whole thing parallels the difference between the ancient philosophical sects of the Stoics and the Cynics. The Stoics thought that all else besides virtue was "indifferent;"

---

25. Philip M. Helfaer, *The Psychology of Religious Doubt* (Boston: Beacon Press, 1972), p. 133.

riches, relations, enjoyments, social status were innocent in themselves, but should they impede the pursuit of virtue, as well they might, then they ought to be discarded. The Cynics regarded the Stoics as compromisers. Virtue, the Cynics insisted, was the only needful thing. *Anything* else was an impediment to virtue, so everything else must go. The Cynics renounced property, jobs, family, money, home, even clothing! The birds of the air and the flowers of the field got along just fine without such entanglements. You don't own possessions; *they* own *you*! So get rid of them. Of course, Watchman Nee did not go that far, but I think he had the same ascetical principle in mind. The "Stoic" Christian says, "If I had to give up so-and-so for God, sure, I'd do it." The "Cynic" Christian says, "If I cherish this or that, it's going to get in God's way, so out it goes!"

Bill Gothard warns the introspective pietist that while "others may; you cannot." Get that? An odd hybrid: fundamentalist relativism, which only goes to show the arbitrary character of this all-devouring self-denial. There doesn't have to be anything wrong or sinful about a thing for your fear to finger it as an idol that must be tossed aside. Chairman Nee says the same:

> And many a time we have to confess that it is not any definite sin that is keeping us from following the Lord to the end. We are held up because of some secret love somewhere, some perfectly innocent natural affection diverting our course. Yes, human affection plays a great part in our lives, and the Cross has to come in there and do its purifying work.[26]

I don't know about you, but I don't like the sound of this!

---

26. Nee, *Normal Christian Life*, p. 253.

But it does explain the zeal of certain young missionaries who have stripped from themselves every personal pursuit or diversion, every hobby or interest except the zeal to bring the gospel to heathens in Darkest Zuphrenia. One wonders if it is not a matter of cognitive dissonance reduction: after all that sacrifice, one can never afford to question whether one might have made a big mistake.

Nee saith:

> How do I distinguish which prompting within me is from the Holy Spirit and which is from myself? [...] [Such neophyte Christians] are trying to look within, to differentiate, to discriminate, to analyze, and in so doing are bringing themselves into deeper bondage. Now this is a situation which is really dangerous to Christian life, for inward knowledge will never be reached. Along the barren path of self-analysis. ... That way leads only to uncertainty, vacillation and despair.[27]

How on earth could Nee have failed to see that he himself was fostering precisely such morbid introspection? I doubt anyone else misses it. In the end, the whispering voice of one's personal savior is nothing more than the internalized norms and neuroses of one's particular church. Jesus becomes the ventriloquist dummy for one's own conscience, which has very likely been flogged to raw hypersensitivity from the pulpit. Ritschl already saw this: "when the practice of monkish self-humiliation is revived, meditation upon sin in general and insistence on the nothingness of the creature become tasks

---

27. Nee, *Normal Christian Life*, p. 236.

which induce a constant tendency to morbid fancies."[28] This sort of devotionalism has got to be one of the prime causes for what William James called the religion of "the sick soul."[29]

Another trap Nee and company set for the unwary pietist is the insistence that the believer, incapable of conjuring his own sanctification, must learn to simply "rest" in Christ, whose indwelling power alone can produce the fruit of the Spirit. Otherwise one is in for continual frustration: "The flesh profits nothing" (John 6:63).

> Living in the Spirit means that I trust the Holy Spirit to do in me what I cannot do myself. This life is completely different from the life I would naturally live of myself. Each time I am faced with a new demand from the Lord, I look to him to do in me what he requires of me. It is not a case of trying but of trusting; not of struggling but of resting in him . . . I shall look to the Spirit of God to produce in me the needed purity of humility or meekness, confident that he will do so.[30]

Anyone who has tried this technique knows well enough that it places one, like a hamster, inside a wheel going nowhere. Why? Well, obviously, because, as Nee admits, this advice goes against one's natural inclination to *try* to do what is necessary, so one must *learn* to do this "resting in Christ," and that ain't easy! So one forever *strives* to rest! The prescription for spiritual frustration turns out only to aggravate the affliction! It's like

28. Ritschl, *Justification and Reconciliation*, p. 162.

29. William James, *The Varieties of Religious Experience: A Study in Human Nature*. Gifford Lectures on Natural Religion, 1901–1902 (NY: Mentor Books/New American Library, 1958), Lectures VI and VII, "The Sick Soul," pp. 112–139.

30. Nee, *Normal Christian Life*, pp. 176–177.

the *Sesame Street* gag where the guy applies some stuff labeled "sunburn lotion," only to be told that it *induces* sunburn!

He Who Hears You Thinks He Hears Me

When pious guru Rick Warren writes, "This is what real worship is all about—falling in love with Jesus," daily "carrying on a continual conversation with him,"[31] he has plunged into the sugary swamp of religious infantilism. Jesus is reduced to an imaginary playmate with whom one may hold imaginary conversations, as when a little girl, plastic plates spread on the plastic table, asks her dolly what she would like for dinner.[32] Psychologist Philip M. Helfaer discusses the case of an evangelical patient whose "contemporary religious beliefs, at core, [were] exactly the same as those he held when he was ten, despite a great deal of sophistication in terms of historical knowledge and theological scholarship. The later sophistication simply surrounds, enclothes, and buffers, as it were, the core beliefs."[33]

Here we see a familiar pattern evident in well-known evangelical apologists and biblical scholars who seek, not to

---

31. Rick Warren, *The Purpose Driven Life: What on Earth Am I Here For?* (Grand Rapids: Zondervan, 2002), p. 96.

32. "the attempt is made in certain circles to produce in young children a love for the Saviour . . . It may be granted that in childhood love to the Saviour is analogous to faith in Christ. The latter, however, is something very serious; the former is playful, for otherwise it would not be within the reach of a child." Ritschl, *Justification and Reconciliation,* p. 599.

33. Helfaer, *Psychology of Religious Doubt* (Boston: Beacon Press, 1972), p. 76.

kill the proverbial mouse with an elephant gun, but rather to *defend* the rodent with heavy artillery. Close scrutiny reveals that the whole superstructure of advanced degrees and scholarly smugness represents not genuine intellectual curiosity but instead a bizarre attempt to legitimatize Sunday School beliefs held on an emotional basis. Evangelical theologian Carl F.H. Henry once boasted that elite Process theologians could waste their breath pontificating their sophistry to their seminary groupies while legions of spiritual seekers flock to Billy Graham Crusades, hungry for the Bread of Life. Henry was as learned a theologian as one could possibly be, and here he is, using Billy Graham as the criterion for true theology.[34]

There is much less to the whole thing, this central pillar of the Christian faith, than meets the eye. Fundamentalists have just never thought the thing through, any more than it occurs to a child to wonder how Santa Claus can visit all the chimneys on the globe in one evening. They seem to conceive of the Risen Jesus as still an individual with a human consciousness, someone with whom one may have a "relationship." But, even sitting at the right hand of God, how can he possibly be carrying on millions of conversations with competing pietists jamming the lines every second of every day? He couldn't do that even if he were one of the fifty-headed giants of Greek mythology! A brilliant *Saturday Night Live* skit depicted Jesus (Phil Hartman) appearing one morning in the kitchen of a Born-Again housewife (Sally Field) and asking her if she could maybe hold off praying about daily trivia like this: "Jesus, be with Timmy as he takes his exams today." There's just too much claim on his attention. But this obvious problem never bothers

---

34. Carl F.H. Henry, *Frontiers in Modern Theology* (Chicago: Moody Press, 1968), pp. 152–153.

Born-Again Christians, which just shows what a mind-game it is.

Albrecht Ritschl's disciple, Wilhelm Herrmann, offered a deeper critique.

> It is not of course difficult for an imaginative person so to conjure up the Person of Christ before himself that the picture shall take a kind of sensuous distinctness, and then the ground is ready for the contemplative love to Christ. Some one thinks he has seen Jesus Himself, and *consequently* begins to commune with Him. But what such a person communes with in this fashion is not Christ Himself, but a picture that the man's own imagination has put together. [...] For ... life is not in this picture, but in the historical Christ. [...] It is not the product of our imagination that has power over us, but that portrait of Jesus the form of which He Himself has fixed in the faith created by Him and handed down to us in the New Testament. [To be sure, there are those who] desire, they say, a personal relation with the Christ who is personally present to them now. [But] this is the presence of Christ which we can *experience* in true communion with God, when His appearance in history comes home to our hearts as the most important thing in all the world.[35]

Herrmann's warning reveals a danger that seems never to occur to evangelical pietists. The more one imagines Jesus Christ communicating and "fellowshipping" with him, the

35. Wilhelm Herrmann, *The Communion of the Christian with God Described on the Basis of Luther's Statements*. Trans. J. Sandys Stanyon. Crown Theological Library (NY: G.P. Putnam's Sons / London: Williams and Norgate, 1906), pp. 281, 282, 283–284.

more the "living" Jesus of his devotional imagination threatens to subsume, displace, and *re*place the historical Jesus. These classical Liberal theologians were optimistic that historical study could produce an accurate portrait of Jesus as he was in ancient Galilee, and the irony they saw in the pietistic "personal relationship" was that it outweighed the only Jesus we can objectively know about. Many evangelicals, both Calvinists and Dispensationalists, reject Pentecostal claims of speaking in tongues and contemporary prophecy on the grounds that they constitute an illegitimate supplement to the biblical canon, essentially no different from the Book of Mormon or the *Course in Miracles*. Why do they not see, as Ritschl and Herrmann did, that for Jesus to "walk with me and to talk with me and to tell me I am his own" amounts to the same darn thing?

Sacred Slogan

To have "a personal relationship with Jesus Christ" is a slogan, a shibboleth. Without it, even though one believes in the incarnation, crucifixion, and resurrection of Jesus and trusts in his grace in order to be saved, one is still a "false Christian" doomed to hell. (I believe I am not exaggerating.) Only a slogan? If not, what is the real content? How is it possible to have a "personal relationship" with an individual of the past? Granting that Jesus rose from the dead and is alive today, how can one "relate" to him as to another flesh-and-blood individual? Everyday relationships between individuals depend upon conversational interaction available by sense impression. Conversations may be carried on at long distances and with time intervals (say, by letter or telephone), but there must be such interaction. Is Jesus available in this way? Obviously not. When someone claims that "I speak to him in prayer; he speaks to me through the words of the Bible," this is really metaphorical. Richard J. Coleman sees the problem here.

> A personal relationship with Jesus is different [from ordinary personal relationships] insofar as we will never have the opportunity to know him in his earthly existence. The relationship must therefore be formed on what we can learn about Jesus secondhand [by reading the gospels] rather than by a firsthand experience; but this is no different from forming a personal relationship with someone by correspondence.[36]

But his solution is inadequate. Correspondence by letter *is* in fact firsthand experience of another in that he is communicating specifically and intentionally with *you*. Coleman's suggestion would also imply the possibility of "personal relationships" with Julius Caesar by reading the *Gallic Wars*, or with Abraham Lincoln by reading Sandburg's biography of him. Coleman has failed to justify the use of "personal relationship" language for the kind of religious experience he means to describe, i.e., an "encounter" with the Jesus of the gospels.

Might a "personal relationship with Christ" imply a spiritual being with whom the Christian is in psychic communication? Several UFO cultists and Spiritualist mediums have claimed that Jesus literally communicates with them via internally "heard" voices. Is this what evangelicals think they're doing? Jesus as a "spirit guide" or "space brother"? Granted, Pentecostals and

---

36. Richard J. Coleman, *Issues of Theological Warfare: Evangelicals and Liberals* (Grand Rapids: Eerdmans, 1972), p. 44.

others sometimes say they have experienced occasional visions of Jesus in which Jesus actually speaks to the individual,[37] but this is not the standard "personal relationship." The fact that such visions are exceptional, as all admit, gives the lie to the standard "personal relationship" language. If all evangelical pietists enjoyed regular audio-visual Christophanies, that would indeed entitle them to claim a personal relationship with Jesus, which in fact they do not have. If they did, I'm afraid we would have to invoke the joke: When you talk to Jesus it's prayer; when Jesus talks to you it's insanity.

No doubt all religious people experience the reassuring presence of a divine providence in their lives, but would that count as a "personal relationship"? I don't think so. It's not that specific. It does not begin to answer to the kind of give-and-take interaction implied in a "personal relationship." Besides, why should such a vague spiritual presence be characterized as "Jesus Christ"?

Some readers may find all this threatening. I seem to be attacking Christianity, but I am not. Please remember, I contend that "personal savior"/"personal relationship" has no basis in the New Testament, any more than television evangelism does, than the Toronto Blessing of uncontrollable Spirit-inspired guffawing does. And without it, one would no longer have to be embarrassed by absurdities such as Jesus simultaneously chatting with millions during their "Quiet Time." Why make your faith and yourself look ridiculous?

---

37. Phillip H. Wiebe, *Visions of Jesus: Direct Encounters from the New Testament to Today* (NY: Oxford University Press, 1997); G. Scott Sparrow, *Sacred Encounters with Jesus* (Allen, TX: Thomas More, 2002); Kenneth Hagin, *I Believe in Visions* (Old Tappan/Spire Books, 1972).

Chapter Two

You Believe in Things You Don't Understand

Though my goal in this book is not to bash Christianity *per se*, I have to admit that this chapter does come perilously close to doing that. I briefly analyze major Christian tenets, indicating ways in which crucial difficulties get papered over by euphemisms about "mysteries" before which reason must abdicate. The result is that, as Stevie Wonder (blind Tiresius?) put it (in his great song "Very Superstitious"): "You believe in things that you don't understand." It does count, I think, as superstition when one agrees to say he "believes" in something that he cannot even define or describe. It's not that one *shouldn't* believe such "things" (can one even call them that?); rather, one *cannot* believe in them and in fact *doesn't*. Such a tenet is thus revealed as a slogan without meaning. This is what makes it superstition: if you must parrot a contentless formula, another name for that is an *incantation*.

Perhaps doctrinal points including the Trinity, the dual natures of Christ, the Atonement, and Predestination may retain their venerable importance for the Christian faith even if they must figure into it in some other way than as objects of cognitive assent. We'll see.

Damnation by Grace

As I understand it, the traditional Catholic and Protestant teaching has been that God in his "grace" (free compassion) has provided the atoning death of Jesus Christ as the means of salvation. (Catholics also regard "grace" as a kind of infused saving force conveyed through the sacraments.) In order to tap into this "saving grace," one must repent of sins and believe in Christ as crucified savior. This means that believing in Jesus Christ (in the sense of trusting him for salvation) is the same thing as receiving the already-offered grace of God. One might have been raised with this religion and taken it for granted, never personally committing oneself to it. And this kind of pat, flat, hollow "belief in Christ" would not coincide with receiving God's grace, but that would be our fault, not God's. Saint Augustine virtually equated God's saving grace with *predestination*, on the grounds that human beings are just plain dead in sin, spiritually inert, incapable of even wanting or seeking salvation. His views on the subject did not become normative for Catholicism, waiting to be revived centuries later by Luther and Calvin.

Calvinists have espoused predestinarianism in various forms. Some held to *Infralapsarianism*, the belief that God chose individuals, not yet in existence, to be saved only once

Adam and Eve had fallen into sin and disobedience (hence "after the Fall-ism"). Had they obeyed God, there would have been no salvation *or* damnation. Salvation *depends* upon damnation, i.e., salvation is *from* damnation, which is the punishment for sin. But does this imply that God did not know what would happen, that he was surprised when Adam and Eve bit that piece of fruit? Uh-oh! No good theologically. So let's suppose God *did* know the outcome in advance. Mustn't that make it meaningless to say he assigned salvation and damnation at a subsequent point? So *Supralapsarians* ("before the Fall-ists") decided that God's decision was already made in advance, which in turn implied that he had actually *caused* the Fall. At the Synod of Dort, Calvinist theologians took it a step further, concluding that predestination means something *had* to happen. And thus the choice of those who would believe and be saved, and those who would not believe and thus be damned was not even a real choice analogous to the ones we mortals make. God's decrees, they said, stemmed inevitably from his eternal and immutable nature. (This is pretty close to Spinoza's Pantheistic doctrine that, Nature being but the visible extension of God, every event that transpires is simply the logical unfolding of the divine Nature.)

The monstrous character of this schema makes God into a devil, creating the majority of his creatures only to serve as kindling in hell. Francis Turretin sought to mitigate this somewhat by suggesting that God did not exactly *force* Adam and Eve to sin. No, all he did was to "pull the plug" on his grace which had hitherto sustained them in their innocence. A pretty dirty trick reminiscent of a comic book story[38] in

---

38. Stan Lee, Jack Kirby, and Vince Colletta, "Clash of the Titans" in *Thor Annual* # 1 (NY: Marvel Comics, 1965).

which the Mighty Thor was about to defeat Hercules in even combat—until Odin decreed that Thor's power level be cut in half! I feel that theology that winds up seriously suggesting such things qualifies as superstition, the fretful worship of a demonic tyrant. Worse yet, it has defined its god, its moral ideal ("Be ye therefore perfect even as your Father in heaven is perfect," Matt. 5:48), as being capable of unthinkable cruelty, thus establishing a precedent for their own possible deeds. "If my God hates those who hate him, I ought to do as my God does, and I will hate them too."[39] But back to predestination.

Augustine's views on predestination evolved from what we call *single predestination* to *double predestination*. At first he figured that God chose some to be saved but just left the rest to their fate, not actually choosing them for hell, just not saving them from it. But then he realized that was a false distinction and that God must have assigned some to salvation, others to damnation. And that this choice was made prior to and independent of anything they *might* do, or that God knew in advance that they *would* do. Uh-oh! This introduced the possibility that one might repent and believe as sincerely as one knew how, yet be lacking God's predestining call, and it is this which becomes the definition of "grace."

Here is a nightmare scenario in which one might be a sincere believer and yet be damned because God has withheld grace. John Calvin did not see the problem. He said that the doctrine of predestination ought to be a great comfort to the Christian, since he must know he need not worry whether he

---

39. Hosea Ballou, *A Treatise on Atonement; in Which the Finite Nature of Sin is Argued, its Cause and Consequences as Such; the Necessity and Nature of Atonement; and its Glorious Consequences; in the Final Reconciliation of All Men to Holiness and Happiness* (Hallowell: C. Spaulding, 1828), p. 55.

were a good enough Christian because his salvation depended on God's election, not the Christian's performance (though a genuine Christian, one of the predestined elect, would of course be trying his best to please his Lord).

But the later Puritans saw what Augustine saw and what Calvin did not: if God's choice is inscrutable and unconditional, there could be no way to ascertain whether one was one of the elect or not! Yeah, you might look at yourself and think, "Well, I do want to serve Christ with all my heart. Doesn't that mean I'm in?" Not so fast, pal! You remember how the choir director seemed so holy—until he was caught molesting kids from the Sunday School? *He* probably thought *he* was a good Christian, too, until his true colors, hitherto unsuspected even by himself, showed through. Hoo boy! This, too, is superstition of a sort, the kind Plutarch had in mind when he said, "The atheist believes there is no God; the superstitious man believes there is but wishes there weren't."

The Hopkinsian Calvinists of the eighteenth century decided to make the best of it. They loved God even if their devotion *were* somehow counterfeit, so they said they would be happy, if it came to that, to be damned to hell and suffer there for the glory of God![40]

I think that Revivalists of an Arminian stripe (Free Will or General Baptists, Methodists, and Pentecostals) inherited the same distinction from Calvinists/Puritans even though they had rejected the Calvinism/Augustinianism that led to

---

40. "The sovereignty of God and the negation of man both reach a terrifying climax here in a vision of the damned themselves joining in the glorification of that same God who has sentenced them to damnation." Peter L. Berger, *The Sacred Canopy: Elements of Sociological Theory of Religion* (Garden City: Doubleday Anchor Books, 1969), p. 75.

it. The Puritans (precisely because of the conundrum of never knowing for sure if you were one of the elect) were always seeking any possible "signs of election," of which worldly success was one. But another was a definite "experience of grace," a conversion experience. If you didn't have it, but were a believer, they'd let you come to church but not take communion (Solomon Stoddard's "halfway covenant"). Well, the Methodist revivalists and Free Will Baptist evangelists rejected predestination, but they still believed in the necessity of a definite, *felt* "conversion experience" or "work of grace," a "heart-warming" experience as Wesley called it. We possess a great number of spiritual diaries, letters, and clinical reports from the nineteenth century which reveal a virtual epidemic of crippling anxiety, depression, and even suicides among Protestant pietists who sought but could not find a definite experience of grace.[41]

Their audience might contain people who just couldn't "get it." They would come forward to the "mourners' bench" and "tarry," waiting for God to send his grace. There were many stories recounting how this or that convert agonized mightily, wrestling with God in prayer, only to find nothing had happened. It was only when he gave up and admitted, "Okay, that's it! I guess I'm damned!"—only once he'd come to the end of his rope, that God's grace hit him! I suppose the distinction such stories seek to make is between emotionally trying to stimulate/simulate the experience and leaving the ground clear for God to act unmistakably. (Zen has the same problem: can you do anything to guarantee *Satori*? Or do you just have to wait for it?)

---

41. Julius H. Rubin, *Religious Melancholy and Protestant Experience in America* (NY: Oxford University Press, 1994).

These stories of frustrated seeking might seem to further the notion that you might be a sincere believer and yet find yourself shut out of God's grace. But then again, the stories imply that such spiritual despair can only be temporary, soon giving way to the grace experience, which implies that it is you yourself who are shutting it out. Are you to emulate these paradigmatic seekers, trudging through the Slough of Despond, their despair ironically proving to be the key to an eventual ecstatic breakthrough? I'm afraid you *can't*, and that's because you can't despair of a successful experience of grace, since you now know the happy ending of the story. So you cannot do what the people in the old stories did. Your mourner's bench despair must be a sham.

A la Freud, Catholics and Calvinists agree that our motives are never pure, and that God requires purity. Lucky for us, he himself provides the requisite purity through Christ. Calvinists say he will adopt the legal fiction of considering our pitiful attempts at good deeds to be good even though they still reek of self-deception and self-seeking ("How big a jewel will I get in my crown for this one?"). Catholics say the believer will gradually *become* actually good and holy because of the increasing infusion of the Spirit through the sacraments. But in both cases, they are saying something I can see as reasonable: there is no real nobility in acts performed, deep down, from selfish motives.

What I find awful is the blanket assumption that non-Christian good deeds *must be* somehow counterfeit or more self-interested than those performed by Christians. It is only believing this that makes it possible for Christians to dismiss Gandhi as damned while declaring Jerry Falwell as saved. They deny up and down that God is (= they are) requiring correct theology, not goodness, for salvation, which would admittedly sound unfair. Why? Because they are denying human goodness is possible! No one *is* good, so no good people will be passed over. Clever, but outrageous! Of course, it is only a theological doctrine that forces/allows them to write off non-Christian altruism and compassion as fake in the first place, not any inductive evidence. So it does all come back to doctrine: only those who share my faith will be saved, and that because they share it, period. The essence of bigotry, if they could only see it! And it surely deserves the epithet coined by E.J. Carnell, "orthodoxy gone cultic."[42]

Their excuse for maintaining belief in damnation is this: God must be *just* as well as *merciful*, or he will be cheating. He will be sweeping sin under the rug. He must deal with sin, make sure it is paid for. He must not be some cosmic bleeding-heart liberal who empties the prisons into the streets from a misplaced sense of compassion.

What made the atoning death of Jesus Christ needful? The penalty for sin had to be taken out of *someone's* hide, someone who belonged to the group owing the debt, and yet an individual who had not himself contributed to the debt. God himself could pay the debt (with his eternal life) but does not owe it. Mankind does owe it but cannot pay it without total destruction. The solution: God becomes a member of mankind via the Incarnation. He bears the sin of his kind, though he himself is not personally implicated. Mankind is henceforth off the hook, though one must still make an individual decision to allow that atonement to avail for him.

The effects will not kick in automatically. Since what is in

---

42. Edward John Carnell, *The Case for Orthodox Theology* (Philadelphia: Westminster Press, 1959), p. 113.

view is an actual transformation of human mortals into (sort of) divine immortals, it is a process with which the individual must cooperate. Now, how do you do *this*? By faith, good deeds, and participation in the sacraments. These things will infuse more of God's sanctifying grace into you.

Cross Purposes

But does any of the proposed explanations of the idea of "Christ dying for our sins" make any sense? C.S. Lewis[43] offers to us that basic faith (shall we call it a "lowest common denomination"?) which is content merely to believe that the Cross of Jesus saves but demands no particular theological explanation of how it saves. Such doctrines are secondary, he urges. Nothing to divide the church over. But, as often with Lewis, he is too facile. There is a deeper problem than Christian factionalism here. Why is there all that debating over cross doctrines? Simply because all of them are beset with severe problems. If any one of them made any sense, everyone would probably be happy to agree on it.

Is it any help to say that Jesus' death was an *expiation*, i.e., that his shed blood cleansed us of sin in the same way that the blood of a helpless, squealing sacrificial animal supposedly washed away the sin of the ancient Israelite? The animal sacrifice idea is itself no more intelligible than the cross business! You

---

43. C.S. Lewis, *Mere Christianity* (NY: Macmillan, 1977), p. 57: "The central Christian belief is that Christ's death has somehow put us right with God and given us a new start. Theories as to how it does this are another matter. A good many theories have been held as to how it works; all Christians are agreed on is that it does work."

are trying to explain one puzzle by means of another.

Is it any better to say Jesus' death is a *penal substitution*, letting John Wayne Gacy go free if Mother Theresa were willing to take his place in the gas chamber? Hardly! What sort of justice is this? If you piously believe this one, maybe you never notice the problem, any more than Gacy would question the propriety of the substitution as he packed his bags and left Death Row behind. Don't look a gift horse in the mouth. But how can it have been "just" to allow an innocent man to take the rap for the crimes of another, even if the innocent party agreed? I think the whole thing is based on a failure of ancient law to distinguish between torts and crimes, as if all you had to do for any offense was to buy your way out of it. And if someone else put up the money in your place, you were free to go. Forget about mercy—this isn't even justice!

Universalist theologian Hosea Ballou,[44] much influenced by Deist Ethan Allen,[45] just could not jettison this doctrine fast enough. Ballou invited us to imagine some guy trying to assassinate the President and failing. He is captured and sentenced to death. But, lo and behold, the President himself asks for his would-be killer to receive clemency, *offering to be hanged in the attempted assassin's place!* Would we, Ballou asks, think any of this to be appropriate, much less just, for a single moment? No freakin' way! It would be morally twisted nonsense!

---

44. Ballou, *Treatise on Atonement*, pp. 79–80.

45. Ethan Allen, *Reason the Only Oracle of Man: A Compendious System of Natural Religion Alternately Adorned with Confutations of a Variety of Doctrines Incompatible to it; Deduced from the Most Exalted Ideas Which We Are Able to Form of the Divine and Human Characters and from the Universe in General* (Bennington: Haswell & Russell, 1784).

How about Athanasius' doctrine that God had to live a truly mortal life (including a death) in order to infuse mortals with his own immortality? Sounds good, but besides the questionable business of picturing immortality like some kind of a permeating grease, this one runs aground on the rock (as Thomas J.J. Altizer[46] noted) that no mortal dies for only a couple of days. This theory would work better if there were no resurrection in the story. Now that would be a real death. As we read it in the gospels, we have a docetic charade.

Gregory of Nyssa formulated a theory whereby Jesus' death was a scam to outwit a kidnapper named Satan, who held the whole (sinful) human race hostage. God the Father knew how much Satan would love to add Jesus' immortal soul to his collection (think of Mr. Scratch with his collection of moths in *The Devil and Daniel Webster*), so he offered to barter Jesus' death for the return of the hostages. Satan fell for it, poor dope, not realizing that he couldn't keep a good man down. Jesus rose from the dead, escaping Satan's domain, and left the poor devil holding the bag. The crass mythological character of this hardly requires comment.

Peter Abelard tried to short-circuit all these theories (and more like them) by saying simply that Jesus' death saves us by demonstrating the love of God. But this is exceedingly lame. How does the mere fact of a death, implicitly one that would otherwise have been avoidable, show love? The death could show love only if dying were the only way to save us. If I jumped in front of a speeding car to get you out of its path, and I died, then my death would indeed show my love for you. But

46. Thomas J.J. Altizer, *The Descent into Hell: A Study of the Radical Reversal of Christian Consciousness* (Philadelphia: Lippincott, 1970).

if you are not in any danger and I say, "Watch this!" and jump in front of a car, I'm just crazy.

Little better is Donald M. Baillie's Neo-Orthodox classic *God Was in Christ*,[47] where he argued that the sufferings of the incarnate Christ boil down to the sentimental truism that there is no forgiveness without a painful cost. The father of the Prodigal Son had to blink back the tears of painful memory in order to accept his wayward son back, is that it? On the contrary, the Prodigal's father hasn't a thought about the past. He runs to embrace his son joyously. Just the way Jesus (before the Last Supper, anyway) says God forgives sinners--freely! As Harnack[48] pointedly asked in his *What Is Christianity?*, are we to imagine that Jesus went about preaching God's free forgiveness to the repentant, only to change the terms of forgiveness as of the crucifixion? Now it seems it took a cross, and that you must believe in a cross. The change must have come as a way of making sense of the death of Jesus: if he had to die for sins, then we must have needed him to die! From "effect" to "cause."

And thus the plethora of bizarre atonement theories. Old Washington Gladden[49] hit the nail on the head: "The figures used by these theologians are so grotesque that it is difficult to quote them without incurring the charge of treating sacred themes with levity." Again he says,

---

47. Donald M. Baillie, *God Was in Christ* (NY: Scribners, 1948).

48. Adolf Harnack, *What Is Christianity?* Trans. Thomas Bailey Saunders. Harper Torchbooks (NY: Harper & Row, 1957), p. 143.

49. Washington Gladden, *How Much Is Left of the Old Doctrines? A Book for the People* (Boston and New York: Houghton, Mifflin and Company, 1899), p. 178.

It is easy to see why these theories have either perished or become moribund. It is because they are morally defective. They ascribe to God traits of character and principles of conduct which are repugnant to our sense of right. It is because men are compelled to believe that the Judge of all the earth will do right, that they cannot believe these theories.[50]

To these morally reprehensible atonement doctrines one must add any doctrine of the cross that leads to the conclusion that people will be damned to eternal torture for not believing in it.

Bultmann recognized the difficulties with rationally explaining the atonement and he saw them as prime evidence for his claim that mythology taken literally contradicts the point the myth itself seeks to make. For example, myth says that God lives up in heaven. In philosophical language, the point would seem to be the transcendence of God. But literally the heaven business implies that God is simply far removed in space,[51] as if he were an alien being living on another planet (which is just what some literal-minded eccentrics have made him! Remember all those books with titles like *God Drives a Flying Saucer!*).[52] So the point is reversed and negated if you

50. Washington Gladden, *Present Day Theology* (Columbus, OH: McClelland and Company, 1912), p. 162.

51. Rudolf Bultmann, "New Testament and Mythology" in Hans Werner Bartsch, ed., *Kerygma and Myth: A Theological Debate*. Trans. Reginald H. Fuller. Harper Torchbooks (NY: Harper & Row, 1961), p. 10, fn 2: "Mythology is the use of imagery to express the other worldly in terms of this world and the divine in terms of human life, the other side in terms of this side. For instance, divine transcendence is expressed as spatial distance."

52. R.L. Dione, *God Drives a Flying Saucer* (NY: Bantam

pause for a second to notice and then to insist on a literal application.

The same goes for the atonement. Bultmann says the point of the myth that a god should come down from heaven, assume human flesh, and die for the sins of mortals, is to say that God forgives by grace, not by any human effort. It's all from his side, not ours. But all these atonement theories assume that there was a literal transaction of some sort on the cross the day Jesus died. And the implications, as we have seen, are absurd. It's like asking how the Pharisees came to be noticing that Jesus dined with publicans and sinners unless they did, too (Mark 2:15–17). How else would they have known? Or why would the woman sweep her whole house by lamplight searching for a lost drachma until she found it--and then blow the money by inviting her neighbors over for a party to celebrate it!? (Luke 15:8–10) You're missing the point.

In the same way, from Bultmann's perspective, the ugly scenario of a supposedly loving Father condemning his innocent but obedient Son to crucifixion is an unintended consequence of the powerful myth of the atoning cross. You're not supposed to take the details literally. Any more than you would ask if the prince and the princess really lived happily ever after--with no quarrels? No money problems?

I once saw the ultimate example of someone following out the atonement myth to its most grotesque extreme. It was an evangelistic tract in which a kid's dad punished him for swearing by making the kid whip his dad with his own belt, insisting on it even when his shocked son quails at the prospect of lacerating his beloved dad. One can hardly imagine Ward and the Beaver in such a kinky scenario. But you have to give

Books, 1973).

the writer credit for being consistently literal. He had followed out the premise of the innocent suffering on behalf of the sinner to its bitter end. And in the process he had proven that this was exactly the wrong way to go!

I guess Bultmann was right. It seems to work pretty well when Billy Graham preaches forgiveness through the cross without digressing into theology lessons about how this might work. The power of the myth shines through the myth only when it is not obscured, ironically, with rationalistic attempts to make it make sense (which it doesn't anyway!).

Or, on second thought, does it work simply because Billy is not letting his buyers get a close look at the product he is selling them? If they thought it all the way through, would they still think it sounded viable? Maybe Bultmann's is really little more than an attempt to cover up the problems with a band-aid. Is his non-theology of the cross any better than those desperate chauvinists who admit Paul's specific arguments against women's equality are fallacious but that we have to accept his conclusion anyway? Accept the conclusion after kicking away all the supports for it?

And has Bultmann forgotten that the whole doctrine of the saving cross arose in the first place as a way to rationalize the scandal of why Jesus died on a criminal's cross? There's the same rationalizing process he laments.

Meet the New Gospel, Same as the Old Gospel

Catholics and conservative Protestants say, "Look, God *is* merciful! He's given you a way *out* of hell! All it entails is admitting you're a sinner, believing in Jesus, etc." Leaving aside the huge matter of whether there is sufficient reason to believe in Jesus, and the injustice of requiring us to believe without sufficient evidence, it seems to me that as long as we are still required to do something, and we are told that, if we don't, we are morally culpable, then nothing fundamental has changed because of the death of Christ. It may be a different set of hoops one is required to jump through, but I thought grace was about no longer having to jump!

It is just such vitiating self-contradictions and logical convolutions that make many of us decide that Christian theology is not so much false as absurd. And for Christians to insist that we believe it by faith, even though there is nothing coherent to believe, is just like the Thought Police officer O'Brien in George Orwell's *1984*: he insists we believe there are three lights when we know there are only two. Otherwise we will not be released from torture. How revealing, then, that theologians tell us that "faith is a gift," or that it is predestined. Aren't they admitting that they wouldn't believe it either if not for the divine hypnosis of "grace"?

Glory Hallelujah, We're Building the Perfect Beast

The Nicene Creed was drafted to resolve the Christological controversy between the Arians (Arius, Asterius, Eusebius of Nicomedia) and the Alexandrians (Bishops Alexander and Athanasius). Neither of their Christological positions was identical with what would later emerge as "orthodoxy."

Athanasius held that Jesus Christ was the Word made flesh (John 1:14). The Word (*Logos*, the creative reason of God, a notion derived from Heraclitus, the Stoics, and Philo) was a separate person sharing the divine nature. The Word is also the Son. The Father begat or generated the Son, but this is a logical, not a chronological priority. They have always been in a relationship of loving interdependence: the Son is "eternally begotten" by the Father, as Origen said. The Word is God's own wisdom through which he created all things (Prov. 8; John 1). In order to save humanity, the Son took on human flesh (not yet understood as a full human nature, just a human body, which will later be considered heresy).

Arius held that Jesus Christ was the incarnation of a heavenly being who had been the very first creature, and through whom as an agent or assistant God had created the rest of the creation (Wis. 8:22; Sir. 1:4; Col. 1:15–16). But he did not share divine nature, the nature of the Father. Both before and during his earthly sojourn he learned wisdom and virtue through discipline and suffering. At the resurrection he was given divine honor and dignity. He was adopted *by grace* as "Son," "Word," "Lord," "Wisdom," even "God," because by his perfection in virtue he had come to participate in these qualities which *by nature* belong to God alone. God's foreknowledge told him from the beginning that Christ would successfully attain this perfection, and so scripture calls Christ "Son," "Word," "God," etc., by anticipation even before his earthly life (e.g., John 1:1; Gal. 4:4).

Arian theologians offered *three scriptural points*. The outline of this schema of Christ being pre-existent in heaven, yet later receiving even greater glory as a reward, is certainly to be found in Philippians 2:5–11 and in the Epistle to the Hebrews. The idea that the pre-existent Word as an agent of creation was himself created can easily be inferred from John 1:1 ("and the Word was divine" or "the Word was a god.")

since the created status of Wisdom is explicit in the texts that clearly form the background of John 1. The notion of Christ's being perfected through endurance and suffering and of his growing in wisdom is certainly found in Luke 2:52 and in Hebrews 2:10.

In addition, they offered *three theological points*. The idea of the Father begetting the Word smacked of Gnostic emanationism. If the Word were eternal, he must be unbegotten, and this would seem to make Christ into God's brother, not his Son! "Eternal generation" is a piece of incoherent sophistry, like a "square circle." And if God is Father *by nature*, and if the Son is Son *by nature*, then God was *forced* to beget the Son, and this is to reject God's sovereignty and freedom.

One sometimes hears people cavalierly dismiss this debate as much ado about nothing, as if the whole thing were over one single letter: *homoousia* versus *homoiousia* ("of the same nature" versus "of like nature"). That's just a joke, and it masks the real irony: the theologians thought they were "unpacking" what was implicit in the concept of Christ, but it is painfully obvious that what they were really doing was *designing* a Christ concept to certain desired specifications, almost like Dr. Frankenstein knitting together the components for his artificial man. (Or, if you prefer a classier analogy, think of the committee-made Pandora, to whom each Olympian god contributed one part.) And that only becomes more clear as we trace the further development of Christology.

Fine-Tuning the Savior

Both sides saw salvation as *theosis*, divinization or deification.[53] Christ had made it possible for us to "become God." (Athanasius said, "God became man so that man might become God.") We could become immortal. By grace, i.e., by adoption, we could become what God is by nature. In order to attain this, we must live a life of faith and good works. This remains the Eastern Orthodox view, where they preach unabashedly the doctrine of *synergism*: we must work with God for our salvation. Athanasius held that Christ must be identified with God in order to make our deification possible. Human nature is mortal/corruptible because it is subject to change and decay (including moral decay, or sin). *Theosis*, deification of human nature, is made possible because in Christ's incarnation the unchanging eternal, divine nature unites with human nature and transforms it essentially. In Christ we experience this transformation. Christ must have been God incarnate, since otherwise the savior could not bring to humanity what humanity needs for deification: genuine deity.

Arius believed that Christ must be identified with creatures in order to make our deification possible: he, precisely as a creature, attains the reward of deification in exactly the same way we do ("the pioneer and perfecter of our faith;" "the firstborn of many brothers") and thus establishes the possibility of deification for the rest of creatures. No chemistry of essences and natures is needed; God simply effects the adoption as sons/daughters by his grace, i.e., by fiat.

---

53. Robert C. Gregg and Dennis E. Groh, *Early Arianism: A View of Salvation* (London: SCM Press, 2012).

Gonna Find Out Who's Naughty or Nicea

At the *Council of Nicea* (325 C.E.), summoned by Constantine, the bishops decided the issue by voting in Athanasius' favor. After the Emperor's death, the decision was reversed, then reversed again, so that the initially victorious Athanasius was suddenly exiled, then recalled! Arian Christology, the belief that Jesus Christ was neither fully God nor man, but a kind of archangel, survived among the barbarian Goths, evangelized by the Arian missionary Ulfilas. They lived in Northern Europe from whence many later relocated to North Africa. Early passages of the Koran seem perhaps to reflect Arian Christology, and many Arian Christians converted to Islam. Today, the major Arian group is Jehovah's Witnesses. Arian Christology has also remained a favorite notion among certain English theologians.[54]

Finding Apollinaris Appalling

The aftermath of the Arian Controversy was the debate over precisely how human Jesus Christ was, granting his full divinity. Athanasius had pretty much taken the humanity of Jesus for granted without defining it. His disciple *Apollinaris* taught what he believed to be the natural implication of Athanasius' doctrine, namely that Jesus Christ had only a human body of flesh and a human soul/mind, but not a human *spirit*. That, he reasoned, must have been "left open" to fit in the divine Logos. After all, it had to plug into the organism *some*place, right?

---

54. Maurice Wiles, *Archetypal Heresy: Arianism through the Centuries* (NY: Oxford University Press, 1996).

He was opposed by three theologians (boyhood chums, now ecclesiastical bigwigs), *Gregory of Nyssa*, *Gregory of Nazianzus*, and *Basil of Caesarea*, all from the Asia Minor province of Cappadocia, hence their collective nickname, the *Three Cappadocians*. These men argued that if Jesus saved us by becoming human, assuming humanity (i.e., taking humanity onto himself), and so raising us to the level of divinity, then in order to save our spirits he must have *had* a human spirit, not just the divine one. What, did he redeem only two thirds of any human being? Their slogan was "What is not assumed is not redeemed." So Jesus Christ must have been fully human as well as fully divine, not half and half like a mythical demigod. Anyway, the *Council of Constantinople* decided this issue in favor of the Three Cappadocians in 381. While they promulgated no new creed, they did beef up the original draft of the Nicene Creed, adding extra material about the Holy Spirit ("the Lord, the giver of life, who proceeds from the Father"), so that the version repeated in churches today is actually the Nicene-Constantinopolitan Creed.

Nesting Instinct

The story goes that Nestorius, Bishop of Constantinople, was disturbed at hearing some of his parishioners praising Mary as the *Theotokos*,[55] "Mother of God." This made him reflect upon the Christological question: how are the divine and human natures of Jesus Christ related? He decided they could not be

---

55. My old pal Mike Shurgan once commented on a tabloid story about a woman who saw the face of Jesus on her freshly-made tortilla: "I guess that's the theo-tacos!"

related in any way that would make it meaningful to call Mary's infant son "God." He is said to have exclaimed, "God is not a baby two or three weeks old!" Imagine the scene at home with the Holy Family: "Mary, cantcha change God's diaper? Joseph, it's time for the Almighty's two o'clock feeding!" In the once-controversial French film *Hail Mary*, which sets the nativity in the modern world, the Holy Family is setting off for a picnic in the country when all of a sudden, out of nowhere, young Jesus announces, to no apparent point, "I am he who is." Joseph's reaction: "Get in the car."

Nestorius was thought to have taught something to the effect that in Jesus Christ there were two subjects, divine and human, perhaps two persons, or something close to this. According to his own rediscovered writings, admittedly not a model of clarity, Nestorius regarded Jesus of Nazareth as "the assumed Man," and there was the divine Word, the pre-incarnate Son of God. By the grace of God they formed one person with two natures. But Nestorius was misrepresented as teaching that Jesus and the Word were two persons sharing but a moral unity.

"Opposing" him (but actually holding to virtually the same view!) was Cyril of Alexandria who argued that Jesus had been one person with two natures (divine and human) and that the personhood was divine, supplied from the divine side, i.e., had there been no mission of incarnation for the Word to undertake, there should have been no Jesus of Nazareth at all. The divine Word forms the nucleus of the Incarnation. This sounds sort of like Apollinarianism, but it isn't, since Cyril readily admitted the human Jesus had a body, soul, *and spirit*. He was fully human, though he wouldn't have existed at all except for his divine destiny. On the other hand, it is not hard to see how Nestorius' position might be taken as opening the door to a kind of adoptionism or separationism. It bothered Cyril and his faction that Nestorians spoke of a "Word/man" Christology, not a "Word/flesh" Christology.

The *Council of Ephesus* decided in 431 in favor of Cyril. Of course this didn't really settle much; the Nestorian churches just picked up their marbles and left for home. Nestorian Christianity still thrives today, especially in Iran. Nestorius had been vilified, made a straw-man against which to define orthodoxy. He did not actually espouse what is called "the Nestorian heresy," nor do today's Nestorians. In fact, one photograph of a gathering of Nestorians shows them holding up a big banner praising the Theotokos!

Monotonous Controversy?

Eutyches, pious Archimandrite of a monastery in Constantinople, tried to explain how the two natures of Christ were related in one person. He admitted that the divine and human natures remained distinct from one another going into the union, until the point of the incarnation occurring via the impregnation of Mary. Afterward, Eutyches ventured, the two natures combined into a single nature (*monos physis*) unique to Jesus Christ. From thereon in Christ has a single nature. One person *from* two natures. The implied analogy is like salt and water: they fuse together into a new, single solution. Those who believe this are known as "Monophysites."

Opposing Eutyches was Pope Leo, among others, Leo being the actual author of the formal response to Monophysitism, *Leo's Tome*. These Dyophysites (believers in two natures) insisted that the two natures remained distinct, inseparably united, not mingled or confused. The proper analogy here would be that of oil and water: pour both into a blender and run it till Doomsday, and the oil is never going to mix with the water, even though not so much as a film of oxygen molecules separates them. The *Council of Chalcedon* decided this one in favor of Leo and his buddies in 451. Again, there was no actual resolution, since the numerous Monophysite churches went their merry way and exist till this very day. The Coptic Church, Ethiopian Orthodox Church, Armenian Orthodox Church, etc., are Monophysite.

Triplethink

In the New Testament we have a few sets of triple formulae: 2 Corinthians 13:14; 1 Corinthians 12:4–6; Galatians 4:6; 1 Peter 1:2; Ephesians 3:14–16.(We must omit the spurious interpolation 1 John 5:7–8, "For there are three that bear witness in heaven, the Father, the Word, and the Holy Spirit, and these three are one.") Here we have what seem to be the seeds from which the later doctrine of the Trinity would blossom. The beginning of the sort of theoretical reasoning involved in the Trinity can be seen in John 14–16, the Johaninne Farewell Discourses.[56] But it is erroneous to claim, as many do, that the Trinity is already present, full-blown, in the New Testament. That is merely the assertion of biblicists who do not feel entitled to any belief not spelled out in the New Testament, and it is why the original Socinians and Unitarians rejected

---

56. Arthur Wainwright, *The Trinity in the New Testament* (London: SPCK, 1962).

Trinitarianism in the Reformation era. But it is more complex than that, as we will shortly see. What this tells us (or *should*) is that we have no more business dogmatizing based on inductive, probabilistic exegesis of a ragtag bunch of scripture texts than we do insisting on a preferred interpretation of an ambiguous text. All we can do is formulate theories and admit the tentative character of them. But that won't be good enough for you if you are obsessed, as religious believers usually are, with certainty. And then you're just kidding yourself, pretending you know when you don't. Here are some of the theories that hardened into dogmas.

Irenaeus at the end of the second century put forth the doctrine of "economic" (or dispensational, or administrative) Trinitarianism. According to this, the three divine persons were first differentiated at creation according to Psalm 33:6 ("By the word of the Lord the heavens were made, and all their host by the breath [*ruach*, "spirit"] of his mouth." Twentieth-century Roman Catholic theologian Piet Schoonenberg[57] made an alternative suggestion, reversing the "enhypostatic humanity" doctrine of Cyril of Alexandria and suggesting instead that the Word first gained its distinct personhood at the incarnation, when it assumed the human being Jesus of Nazareth. The personhood was contributed by the human side, not by the divine, as traditionally believed, and this implies there was no plurality of persons in the Godhead till the incarnation. The Word and the Spirit had been simply aspects of God till then.

Marcellinus of Ankyra in the fourth century developed economic Trinitarianism in the direction of *successive*

---

57. Piet J.A.M. Schoonenberg, *The Christ: A Study of the God-Man Relationship in the Whole of Creation and in Jesus Christ* (NY: Herder and Herder, 1971).

"economies" or "dispensations" of the Logos: first in creation, second in the incarnation, and third in the outpouring of the Spirit at Pentecost. At the Second Coming, he taught, the Logos will again be absorbed into God, and "God will be all in all" (1 Cor.15:28).

Tertullian in the early third century, in Carthage, introduced the terminology of "three persons, one essence," but by *persona* he meant something like "faces" or "masks" like the ancient actors wore to signify their roles. His meaning might be developed in various ways. Sabellius later in the third century put forth the doctrine of *Modalism* (or Patripassianism ["the Father suffers-ism"] or Theopascism ["God suffers-ism"]) which can be seen as a development of Tertullian's ideas. Sabellius said that Father, Son, and Holy Spirit are three *modes* in which God manifests himself, not three persons within the Godhead. The famous "ice-water-steam" analogy fits Modalism.

The Three Cappadocians in the fourth century experimented with slightly different terminology: three substances (existences), one essence. This is very close to what became orthodox dogma: "three persons in one essence."

The Councils of Nicea and Constantinople affirmed that the Son and the Spirit were of the same (not just similar) nature with the Father. The later Athanasian Creed made this even more explicit.

Augustine of Hippo in the late fourth century thought of the Trinity in terms of *relations* within a person or between persons. He pictured the Trinity as analogous to memory, intellect, and will or to lover, beloved, and love. The later controversy between Eastern and Western churches over the addition of the clause *filioque* ("I believe in the Holy Spirit, the Lord, the giver of life, who proceeds from the Father *and from the Son"*) to the Nicene-Constantinopolitan Creed is relevant here, since one reason the East rejected it was that they thought having the Spirit proceeding from both Father and Son but not proceeding from the Spirit (himself) denigrated the equality of the Spirit with the other two persons. They suspected Western (Augustinian) Trinity analogies did the same by implying that, while the Father and the Son were persons, the Spirit was some kind of impersonal force passing between them.

Roscellinus of York in the eleventh century argued that to speak of "essence" is just to talk about what kind of thing something is, what *category* to place it in. The result when applied to the Trinity is that there are three Gods—Tritheism, as implied in the well-known "three light bulbs" analogy.

Gregory of Nyssa had already tried to head this objection off by saying that "Godhead" refers to the divine operations or roles, not to nature or essence at all. Jehovah *rules* as God. He is *enthroned* as God. The three persons, Father, Son, and Spirit, all reign as God. And they are of the same nature, just as all human beings are of the same nature with each other and technically ought to be called "man" collectively, never "men" plurally. Granted, we define individuals by their operations of roles, too, and if many do the same thing, we do properly use plurals denoting their roles, like "many orators," "many physicians." They may be distinguished from one another in this way because their work is parallel to or even competitive with one another's. But in the case of God, every act is performed conjointly by all three persons harmoniously, each performing his own function in the performance of the one task, e.g., to save. Thus one cannot distinguish them as "gods" as one could Apollo, Hermes, and Hera, who are (false) gods dividing the labor and doing different things. (I am not so sure this works;

I think Gregory reads too much into the joint efforts of the members of the Trinity; is this the only reason we may not call them three Gods?)

The "Personality" of the Holy Spirit

Whence comes the idea of the "personality of the Holy Spirit"? The Worldwide and International Church of God movements (the churches of Herbert W. Armstrong and Garner Ted Armstrong respectively) hold to *binitarianism*, which is like Trinitarianism except that it rejects the personality of the Spirit. Others consider them heretics for it. Where did the idea come from? The Bible seems not to speak of personality in connection with the Spirit except insofar as the Spirit bears the personality of Christ to us. The "person" or "substance" idea of Tertullian and the Cappadocians does not suggest anything quite so specific in meaning as our modern notion of "person" or "personality." Nor even does Augustine's analogy of relations within a person. "Person" was defined more in our sense, and applied to the Trinity, by Boethius in the sixth century. Henceforth "person" denotes at least an individual center of rationality.[58]

It seems to me that the Nicene bishops fabricated a third Christian God by means of abstract theological deduction. The

---

58. See Hermann Gunkel, *The Influence of the Holy Spirit: The Popular View of the Apostolic Age and the Teaching of the Apostle Paul*. Trans. Roy A. Harrisville and Philip A. Quanbeck II (Philadelphia: Fortress Press, 1979) and Hendrikus Berkhof, *The Doctrine of the Holy Spirit*. The Annie Kinkead Warfield Lectures, 1963–1964 (Richmond: John Knox Press, 1967).

notion that the Holy Spirit is a person in whatever sense that the Father and the Son are strikes me as grossly artificial.

Hindu Trinitarianism?

Hinduism, too, has a Triad of divine persons: Brahma the Creator, Vishnu the Preserver, and Siva the Destroyer. Historically, this formula appears to be a theological compromise position, an attempt to reconcile the two great factions of Hindu worship, Saivas and Vaisnavas. Brahma's worship was antiquated by this time, so why was he included? My guess is that adding him to the formula took the theological tension out of the thing. One need not ask, as would be natural if there were only two persons in the Godhead, which "one" has the priority over "*the* other" if there are three.

The analogy to Christian theology is not quite exact, since the Hindu version is really a case of "economic Trinitarianism." Behind the three great Gods lies an all-embracing Brahman, the Godhead itself, which is prior to and more real than the individual divinities. Christian Trinitarianism doesn't say that, because that tends to relativize the persons into mere roles, appearances, a sort of "docetic" Trintarianism of seeming persons who are not ultimately real. Then what you've got is Modalism.

Remember, just because a doctrine involves "threeness" in some fashion doesn't mean it is Trinitarianism. What makes it Trinitarianism is the precise way the nature of the three entities is understood, as well as how they are thought to relate to one another. This is why you cannot point to New Testament formulas like "in the name of the Father and of the Son and of the Holy Spirit" and say it teaches Trinitarianism. No, it is just part of the data that raises the question to which Trinitarianism is one answer, Modalism is another, and Tritheism is yet another.

Mystery or Mystification?

Does the Trinity make any sense? Defenders of the doctrine have always admitted that their formulations are not explaining what it means so much as erecting a barrier (a la the *Via Negativa*) to protect the deep truth of the Trinity from the rude and over-simplistic attempts of impatient mortals to whittle it down to some idol they may satisfactorily understand. "Not so fast, mister! There's more to it than you think! Best to fall silent and bask in the Mystery!"

Rationalist theologians like Universalist Hosea Ballou have rejected this, saying that the Trinity is merely a bad theory, and that theologians are just spin doctors trying to cover their butts, making a bad theory look good. Want proof? Ask individual Christians what they think the Trinity means. You will invariably get some sort of Modalism or Tritheism, not real Trinitarianism, though no one seems to know the difference! And what else can they do? There would seem to be no middle option between the two "heresies" where the would-be orthodox mind may settle down. If you want to believe in anything, if you want to have some sort of notion in your mind, you are going to "round it off" to one of the options you can understand. Let's put it this way: when the professed Trinitarian prays, the "mental motions" he goes through as he directs his prayers to the various Persons of the Trinity are identical to those of an outright polytheist who directs prayers now to Zeus, now to Apollo, now to Athena, or perhaps first to Siva, then Ganesha, then to Kali. I think Jewish and Islamic critics of Christianity are right: Christians would like to be considered monotheists (and would like so to consider themselves), but they don't deserve the appellation. It's as if a Mormon gladly admitted having many wives but also claimed he was a monogamist.

Theologians including Bultmann, Tillich, and Schleiermacher have suggested that superstitious thinking and speaking about God stem from a mythological (i.e., objectifying) God concept, making him into a being among beings rather than the Ground of Being, or Being-itself. But is there an approach to Trinitarian faith compatible with a suitably transcendent understanding of the "God beyond God"? For my money, Vladimir Lossky[59] shows the way past superstition.

> Our thought must be in continuous motion, pursuing now the one, now the three, and returning again to the unity; it must swing ceaselessly between the two poles of the antinomy, in order to attain to the contemplation of the sovereign repose of this threefold monad. How can the antinomy of unity and trinity be contained in an image? How can this mystery be grasped save by the aid of an idea—be it that of movement or that of development—which is inadmissible?

Lossky advocates *apophatic* theology, the *via negativa*. In other words, God surpasses human understanding and

59. Vladimir Lossky, *The Mystical Theology of the Eastern Church* (Crestwood, NY: St. Vladimir's Seminary Press, 1976), p. 46.

therefore is not susceptible to being captured or expressed in rational, conceptual thought. At best, one can but peel away inadequate concepts of God (a redundancy). One can become less wrong, less idolatrous, less superstitious. What of the positive? It is "rising above rational concepts" to pure immersion in the indescribable Godhead. I should say that the three persons of the Trinity, precisely *because* of the mutual contradiction between the three and the one, function like Zen koans, insoluble riddles aiming at derailing the locomotive of reason, making the mind jump the track, leaving behind the reliance upon concepts that pretend to reveal God but only manage to substitute for "him."[60] And this is what distinguishes the mental process described by Lossky from what I have described as *de facto* polytheism.

Is the Trinity a divine Mystery beyond human ken? Or is it just a bad theory? More mystification than mystery? I don't know. But critics[61] charge that the real meaning of the doctrine of the Trinity is this: "*Sit down and shut up!*" That is, it is specifically designed to cut off thought and cow believers into intimidated submission to Mother Church. "I give up! Go ahead and tell me what to believe! I don't get it, but whatever it means, I'm confident the bishops are right!" This is second-hand "belief." But how can you "believe" in X? "You believe in things you can't understand. . . . Very superstitious. . . ."

---

60. Meister *Eckhart: A New Translation*, Fragment 30: "It is God's nature to be without a nature. To think of his goodness, or wisdom, or power is to hide the essence of him, to obscure it with thoughts about him," pp. 243–244.

61. Specifically my friend Grover Furr.

Chapter Three

My God Is Fear[62]

Dancing on the Griddle

Suppose a man proposes marriage to a woman. He tells her he loves her and wants to do great things for her. And, just to sweeten the deal, he pulls a gun on her and threatens to blow her pretty head off if she turns him down. Absurd as it sounds, absurd as it *is*, things like this have happened—because there are dangerously insane people out there. Is one of them named "Jehovah"? It kind of sounds like it when we are told that God loves us more than tongue can tell and that if we turn down his gospel of salvation he is going to consign us to eternal torture. It is a case of what Paul Watzlawick calls the "'Be Spontaneous'

---

62. "Fear, nothing else. That is . . . my God." Nikos Kazantzakis, *The Last Temptation of Christ*. Trans. P.A. Bien (NY: Bantam Books, 1961), p. 142.

Paradox,"[63] where some action or feeling is *commanded* despite the fact that, by nature, it must arise *freely*. It is a cruel joke, rendering the mandated behavior impossible. What, God doesn't know this? It is easier to imagine that a bunch of bone-headed bishops and theologians didn't know it or felt it was worth fostering an absurdity or two if the terror of it could keep the suckers in line.

"Oh no!" say the defenders of the faith, the sacred spin-doctors. "We were already in trouble, having sinned against God and buying our own asbestos ticket to the Inferno. God is throwing us a life preserver so we won't drown in the Lake of Burning Sulfur!" Yeah? And who was it, pray tell, who decided we deserved hell in the first place? The angry Jehovah, *that's* who! Everything about this is not only absurd but reprehensible. Is the damning decree possible for a just deity? I mean, who could possibly deserve *eternal torment*? I dare say that not even Hitler could deserve that. Such a God pretty much *is* Hitler. Call it the *Hellocaust*.

And is it at all thinkable that a loving Heavenly Father could subject his wayward creatures to such treatment? If you say yes, you are stretching the definition of "love" so far as to turn it into its opposite. Better forget it.

One more thing: since God is supposed to be compelling sinners to roast in hell, obviously, against their will, why doesn't he instead *enlighten* and *sanctify* them? Imagine: upon their demise, the sinners snap out of it. "What was I thinking? How stupid could I have been? Thank God; he's caused the scales to fall from my eyes! Hallelujah!" Not a bad scenario, is it?

---

63. Paul Watzlawick, *How Real Is Real? Confusion, Disinformation, Communication* (NY: Vintage Books, 1977), pp. 19–21, 216.

Some seek to avoid that possibility, suggesting that sinners *choose* to go to hell. That is so stupid as to require no refutation. Granted, plenty of people choose not to repent, not to accept the gospel, but of course no one actually prefers to go to hell. They don't think here is a hell to go to. They didn't believe in Christ, so why should hell-belief seem more plausible to them?

It only gets perverse when Christians try to mitigate the prospect of a fiery pit of torment by half-demythologizing it, psychologizing it. They suggest that the "torment" of hell will simply be inconsolable regret for not having repented before it was too late. This is too rich! Let me get this straight: up on earth, these sinners didn't give a hoot about God, *but now they do!* Now they heartily wish they could bask in the Beatific Vision. And God just gives 'em the finger? Death, then, immediately sanctifies them, imparting a longing for God, which does them no good. Ludicrous.

All in all, when Christianity wields the stick as well as the carrot, threatening damnation for those who spurn the message, it must be dismissed as the height of superstition. Universal salvation, i.e., Jesus died to save humanity, *and it worked*, would at least not be superstitious, whether true or not.

What the Heck?

The history of hell is the refutation of hell. We can trace the gradual evolution of the hell concept. The Old Testament knows nothing of it, instead positing either just plain death (Gen. 3:19) or the Babylonian shadow realm of Sheol to which all must go, good or evil (Isa. 14:9–20).[64] The Old Testament does know of a

---

64. As when Han Solo ignores a soldier's warning about the

fiery netherworld, the realm of Molech,[65] opening at the foot of Mount Zion. This was Tophet, Gehenna, the place where living infants were offered in sacrifice. But it was not yet thought of as a place of postmortem punishment for the wicked. During the Hellenistic period, Judaism adopted the Greek Tartaros, the deep cavern where Zeus had confined the rebellious Titans. In Judaism, the Titans were replaced by the Watchers, the fallen angels. But even this was not yet a fiery hell. That element was apparently derived from the preaching of Neo-Pythagorean missionaries who got the idea from the volcanic geography of their homeland in Sicily and Italy.[66] The truth does not grow in such a fashion. Myths do. And if the danger of hell was always there, always real, why do we not hear of it till so late in the day? Though the superstitious character of hell-belief seems overwhelmingly obvious, the idea of eternal torment remains so daunting that even very intelligent, sophisticated individuals feel it would be wiser not to take the risk of incurring it. They still believe in it almost as if denying it would itself constitute a hanging offense.

And besides, is there really an eschatological insurance

---

plummeting temperature and is about to ride out into the tundra in search of Luke Skywalker. He replies, "See you in hell!" He's one of the good guys, willing to sacrifice his life to rescue a friend, yet he expects to wind up in hell, where, therefore, he assumes everybody goes (*The Empire Strikes Back*).

65. John Day, *Molech: A God of Human Sacrifice in the Old Testament*. University of Cambridge Oriental Publications No. 41 (NY: Cambridge University Press, 1989), "The Fires of Molech and Gehenna," pp. 52–55.

66. Peter Kingsley, *Ancient Philosophy, Mystery, and Magic: Empedocles and Pythagorean Tradition*. Clarendon Paperbacks (NY: Oxford University Press, 1995), pp. 192–194, 210–211.

policy to be had? If one fears reprisals for not embracing Christianity, one is far from being out of the woods. By accepting the Christian gospel you are *ipso facto* buying a ticket to one or more Islamic, Buddhist, or Hindu hells! If you're going to be afraid of hell, there's no escape that way! The religions you *didn't* accept might be right, and you're headed for *their* hell!

Perhaps the most damning (no pun intended) aspect of hell-belief is that it retards moral growth by making it impossible for the hell believer ever to grow beyond the crudest, most infantile "morality." "Keep your hand out of the cookie jar, or mommy's going to spank you!" A doctrine that retards moral growth simply cannot be taken seriously, any more than one that promotes bigotry.

We just cannot cripple ourselves by disregarding our better judgment and basing our beliefs on fear. The recurring "What ifs" must be recognized for what they are: what we as Christians called temptations: insidious whispering voices bidding us do the wrong thing. We must stand our ground and refuse to give in! Only so can we ever arrive at "a spirit of power, love, and a sound mind." The voices will die away after a while. There is no reason to take them seriously, and we must ever remind ourselves of that.

These are some of the things that make me dismiss the notion as not plausible enough to worry about. Sure, it *might conceivably* be true, but you could say the same for, say, the crazy belief that the government has been infiltrated by reptilian space aliens. What are the chances?

The Deep Things of Satan

There is great fear of Satan among evangelical believers, more than one might expect given the belief that Christ has effectively triumphed over him (1 John 4:44, "Greater is he who is in you than he who is in the world."). Who and what is the devil? As with the belief in hell, it is crucially important to understand the evolution of the doctrine, for once it stands revealed, it may not be so daunting. It might even be revealed as, dare we say it, superstition.

The Satan character began as a special son of God or angel in charge of divine sting operations. The Satan (at first it wasn't even a proper name, but a noun meaning "the Adversary" in the sense of a prosecuting attorney) was so zealous for the honor of his Lord that he kept close tabs on mortals and was quick to sniff out any whiff of pretense on the part of God's ostensible servants. What was their *real* motivation? Let's find out! So the Satan would mount a scenario to "try men's souls." Was Job really as pious as his reputation would suggest? Try taking away his material wealth, his family, then his bodily health and see if he's *still* such a big fan of the Almighty. Is King David's reliance on God's mighty arm absolute, or does he have back-up plans in case God disappoints him? Maybe whisper in his ear that it might be prudent to take a census of available soldiers?

Obviously all this is completely mythological. And that's not just compared with modern, materialistic science. No, there is a far more serious clash with *theology*: the scenario of a deity sitting on his throne up in the sky, surrounded by a flock of godlings including a special agent in charge of security— it is sheer, polytheistic myth. Is that the God you believe in? No, of course your God-concept is defined (or *re*defined) by the philosophical reasonings of Saints Augustine, Anselm, and Aquinas, even if you've never heard of them. You're kidding yourself if you think you're getting your God straight out of the Bible. It's far from being that simple. Do you believe "God" needs an intelligence agency? Isn't he supposed to be omniscient? You take that for granted as "baked into" the very definition of God, but the Bible writers sure didn't. But back to Satan.

Don't both Isaiah chapter 14 and Ezekiel chapter 28 describe the fall of the Archangel Lucifer? No, they don't. Isaiah 14 is a satirical lament celebrating the fall of the king of Babylon, comparing the once arrogant monarch to the godling Helal, son of the dawn goddess Shahar. He was the subject of an astronomical allegory. Helal was the personification of the planet Venus, "the morning star," brightest object in the morning sky—until the mighty Sun rises and blots out the inferior brightness of the planetary upstart. In the story Helal foolishly aims at supremacy in the heavens but is slapped down by Elyon, the Most High. It was a way of describing, in cartoon form, what happened every morning. There were many such astral myths. But Isaiah applies it to the humbling of an earthly tyrant. Satan is not in view at all.

Ezekiel does something quite similar, applying a version of the story of Adam's Fall. At first Adam dwelt in shining glory as God's viceroy, his "signet ring." Like the Tree of Life and the Ark of the Covenant, Adam was assigned a guardian cherub. But Adam grew proud of his glory as the image of God, whereupon he was kicked off the Cosmic Mountain of God.[67] Ezekiel says the same thing happened with the once glorious maritime

---

67. Margaret Barker, *The Gate of Heaven: The History and Symbolism of the Temple in Jerusalem* (London: SPCK, 1991), pp. 71, 101.

trading empire of Tyre. No devil here. These two passages were only later reinterpreted as accounts of the Fall of Satan.

Satan became a villain subsequent to the massive Persian (Zoroastrian) influence on post-Exilic Judaism. Jewish thinkers saw the utility of the Zoroastrian concept of Ahriman, the nefarious anti-god responsible for all the evil in the world. That would seem to get God off the hook! So the once-innocent Satan was retconned as a Jewish Ahriman. But not consistently; Ahriman was pretty much equal and opposite to Ahura Mazda, the good deity. But, on second thought, Jewish thinkers didn't want to sacrifice monotheism, which they would have to do if they duplicated the dualism of Zoroastrianism. So they half-assed it, making their Ahriman analogue, Satan, inferior to Jehovah, an angel created by him. But in doing this, they subverted the whole attempt at theodicy: now God was still on the hook for evil, since of course he had created Satan in the first place. But at least it put some distance between God and the blame.

We do not find the familiar Satan story in the Old Testament. So where *does* it come from? Largely from apocryphal texts written, roughly, between the Testaments, where much attention was given to the story of *Genesis 6:1–4*, where the Sons of God mate with mortal women and beget the Nephilim, mythical ancestors of the Anakim, a Canaanite people of great stature (Num. 13:28, 32–33; Deut. 3:11; 2 Sam. 21:15–22). Originally there was nothing sinister about this. It was simply an ethnological myth designed to account for the comparatively great height of these people (six and a half feet!). But as Judaism grew closer and closer to monotheism, the lesser deities, or Sons of God, had to be recast as evil angels. The story was repurposed, the cohabitation of gods and mortal women made into the cause for the corruption that necessitated the Flood of Noah. As such, the compiler of Genesis sandwiched it between the introduction of Noah and the Flood story proper. No Satan yet, but he will soon be added to the story.

In *1 Enoch VI, VII, VIII* we are explicitly told that the Sons of God, or Watchers, seduced women, then taught them cosmetics and arts of seduction in order to seduce mortal men, poor creatures, to sin. The story teller assigns them a ringleader called Semjaza, who is presumably the same as Satan. The *Testament of Reuben 5:5–7* turns it around. Now the women seduce the Sons of God! The *Book of Jubilees 10:11* makes Satan (here called Mastema, unless that's yet *another* devil) one of the demons, sons of the Watchers who fell. Ten per cent of them are assigned to help him in his appointed task to punish men. The rest are, like the evil Titans of Hesiod's *Theogony*, imprisoned far underground.

Yet another version of the story meets us in *1 Enoch 54*, where the sin of the Watchers was to swear allegiance to Satan, not one of their number but already an evil being in his own right. The *Apocalypse of Moses 16–17* merges the Genesis 6 story of the Sons of God with the Genesis 3 story of the Garden of Eden, retaining the element of sexual seduction. Now for the first time the serpent is made the innocent dupe, as it were, the demon-possessed mouthpiece of Satan to tempt Eve to sin. In fact it is sexual seduction. And she goes on to seduce Adam into sin. The *Life of Adam and Eve 12–17* explains Satan's motive for this act: he had refused to bow down and do homage before the newly created Adam, so God expelled him from heaven. Satan then decided to show how right he had been about humanity by tempting Adam and Eve. We also find this version in the *Koran 7:11–27*.

Second Enoch 18:3 (in some manuscripts where "Satanil" is listed as the leader of the fallen angels) approaches most closely to the Christian version of Satan. Here he had sought to usurp God's throne in primordial times. His temptation of Eve in Eden is just part of his typical evil-doing. "Satanil" means "enemy *of God.*"

Both the original Satan concept, the heavenly prosecutor and master of sting operations, and the Zoroastrian evil anti-god, survive side by side in the New Testament, where he's most often depicted doing his old job, testing the servants of God, to see what they're made of, as when Satan meets Jesus in the desert and asks if he'd want to change rocks into rock candy, leap tall buildings in a single bound, and swear fealty to him instead of God. He seems to be putting Jesus, newly crowned Son of God, through his paces. Similarly, at the Last Supper Jesus tells Peter he and the disciples have stormy weather ahead: "Satan has demanded to sift you all like wheat" (Luke 22:31). That is, he demands his rightful prerogative to put these men, with their protestations of undying loyalty, through the ringer, to see what they're really made of—just like he did with Job. Even in Revelation he is called "the accuser of the brethren," his old historic role.

The point of all this is that we can observe the progress of how the Christian devil grew and transformed as many scribes, pseudonymous writers, and anonymous tale-spinners gradually contributed to the making of a fictional character. We are not talking about a biography of a historical figure but rather the gradual compiling of a mythical one.

Fiendish Fifth Wheel

What difference does the devil really make? He is more of a scapegoat than anything else, it seems to me. Suppose Satan, as one usually hears, is the mastermind of evil in the world, e.g., in the movie *Devil's Advocate*. Satan as a cosmic George Soros? Isn't this a pretty optimistic view of the world? Like, if we could only take this guy out, everything would be okay? Shortly after the 1978 Jonestown horror I was discussing it with a professor at Gordon-Conwell Theological Seminary. He asked, rhetorically, "Bob, don't you think this is a real display of the power of Satan in the world?" I replied, "No, I only wish it *were*! I'm afraid Jonestown shows what human nature is all too capable of."

James 4:1–2 asks, "From whence come wars and fightings among you? Come they not hence, even of your lusts that war in your members? Ye lust, and have not: ye kill, and desire to have, and cannot obtain: ye fight and war, yet ye have not, because ye ask not." What's missing? The devil is conspicuous by his absence. Ever since comedian Flip Wilson's "The devil made me do it" skit, most people have probably felt too embarrassed to invoke this excuse, though it is occasionally offered as a courtroom defense by murderers who are too stupid to think of anything else. But isn't the whole conception of Satan as the Lord of Evil "the devil made me do it" writ large? "Oh no, the Holocaust can't be blamed on human nature! It must be the devil's work!" Is that so? As long as you lay the blame on an invisible, intangible villain, you may not take the real roots of evil seriously enough. And insofar as you do blame such a nefarious spook, shouldn't you recognize it as superstition?

The tendency to sniff out Satan's designs behind every temptation represents an unnoticed theological dualism. As in the *Omen* movies, Satan appears both omniscient and omnipresent. Where is he not active? If it is Lucifer tempting every dieter to sneak that piece of chocolate cake, he must be more ubiquitous than Santa Claus on Christmas Eve. One very frequently hears that "Satan tried to get me depressed" or "Satan whispered this or that to me." "Once you get serious with God, Satan will make you his target." Really? Satan himself? In the film version of *The Exorcist* Father Karras is initially skeptical about the reality of Regan's possession because he is told she is possessed by Satan himself. Isn't that a delusion of grandeur, like thinking you're Napoleon? But the attribution of every temptation to Satan is a delusion of Satan's grandeur. He has gone back to his roots as the anti-god Ahriman.

I hesitate to invoke notorious cartoonist Jack Chick as the poster boy for fundamentalist superstition, but it is really not unfair, given the very widespread use of Chick's cartoon booklets in evangelism. And Chick's publications foster belief in a paranoid cosmos where the ole devil is responsible for the invention of the Roman Catholic Church, the Communist Party, Nazism, the Ku Klux Klan, rock music, liberal Protestantism, Dungeons and Dragons, Darwinism, and the Revised Standard Version. Satan, in short, is everywhere, behind everything non-fundamentalist. Such religious paranoia is extreme but not at all rare.

Satan also plays the role of the boogeyman. Fundamentalists warn those considering a practice of meditation that calms the mind and quiets rushing thoughts, not to do it because Satan might jump into the vacuum thus created. Similarly Calvinist radio host Harold Camping was not alone in condemning

Pentecostal glossolalia as demon-inspired. Poor dumb Pentecostals *think* they are getting "filled with the Sprit" when they speak in tongues, but they are "really" brimming over with Satan!

Historically, fundamentalist leaders have discouraged students from fairly considering opposing theological views or arguments against faith, lest "Satan plant the seeds of doubt." Such warnings presuppose that the devil might hypnotize the listener. Such an attitude only reveals a lack of confidence in one's own faith, even a tacit admission that reason has nothing to do with one's religious beliefs. As Martin Luther called her, reason is seen as "the devil's whore." This is not superstition? This stance is, fortunately, far less common these days; evangelical leaders are well aware of the ready availability of opposing arguments on the Internet. They now make a real effort to address the arguments, often sponsoring public debates. They might rather simply shield the lambs from disturbing ideas, but that has become impossible. Of course, apologetics are by no means new, but they have historically been aimed at reassuring believers that they have nothing to worry about.

Perhaps the most obvious appeal to superstitious dread inculcated by fundamentalist Christianity is the *cautionary tale*, many of which come from the books of Lutheran "expert" on the occult, Kurt Koch.[68] As if whispering to scouts around a campfire, Koch shares harrowing tales of what happened

---

68. Kurt Koch, *Between Christ and Satan* (Grand Rapids: Kregel Publications, 1983), Chapter Four, "Occult Literature," pp. 131–141. Above, I have suggested that superstitious fear has restored Satan to his original status as a virtually omnipotent anti-God. Accordingly, Koch apparently regards these occult grimoires as no mere books, but as genuine counterparts to the God-inspired Bible, only inspired by Satan.

when this one or that one made the mistake of harboring (not necessarily even *reading*!) a copy of *The Sixth and Seventh Books of Moses* or the *Fiery Dragon* or other petrifyingly tedious compilations of medieval gibberish. Spiritual depression, suicidal urges, and sinus headaches followed! "Men, don't let *this* happen to *you*!" Superstition? What other word will do?

Chapter Four

The Neurosis Testament

Sigmund Freud said, "Religion would thus be the universal obsessional neurosis of humanity."[69] A neurosis is a crippling fixation on an outmoded pattern of childish behavior that gets in the way of living life as an adult. Religion is just the childish belief that your parents could do anything you asked, protect you against everything, and answer every question, and that their word was law. We lose that sense of security as we grow up and sooner or later come to realize, with greater or lesser alarm, that our parents are by no means infallible. They taught us the best they knew, but they didn't know as much as we thought they did. This realization need not and should not occasion a crisis. Our new perspective on their human limitations is actually the flip side of our own emerging intellectual and moral autonomy.

---

69. Sigmund Freud, *The Future of an Illusion*. Trans. W.D. Robson-Scott (Garden City: Doubleday Anchor Books, 1964), pp. 70–71.

To accept the fact of their fallibility is to accept our own ability to do *our* best, too, imperfect as it may turn out to be. But many cannot bring themselves to do without a set of infallible parents, so they are relieved to be able to replace Mom and Dad with a Heavenly Father and, if you're a Roman Catholic, a Holy Mother. Such believers, imagining that infallible guidance and omnipotent protection are still to be had from on high, actually from the gods' self-appointed spokesmen, can comfort themselves in the short run even though in the long run, they will receive no better advice or protection than the atheist does. But at least the atheist does not carry the extra burden of having to explain how "God" failed to do a good job. But more on that particular mind-game later.

Possibly the clearest example of religion-fostered neurosis to the point of superstition is the pietist principle of "up to the minute confession" of sins. One must see "the importance of keeping short accounts with God over known specific sins."[70] As explained by a legion of fundamentalist preachers and devotional writers, this means that, as soon as one commits a sin, even a moment's unkind thought, one must suspend one's train of thought to confess the sin to God and ask forgiveness. Why the urgency? The fear is that unconfessed sins, until dealt with, will accumulate, making the Christian less and less sensitive to the leading of the Holy Spirit. And that of course must lead to more sinning. But what does "up to the minute confession" lead to? Endless distraction, just like the constantly jolting electrical headbands assigned to all citizens in the film *Harrison Bergeron*, where they are designed to make it impossible to think deeply or to pursue a complex train of thought.

---

70. Nee, *Normal Christian Life*, p. 202.

An apt metaphor for the dreaded degradation of spiritual sensitivity from failing to confess promptly would be the Jainist belief that one's sins slowly form a quasi-physical "karma body," a metaphysical cement overcoat.

In the early 1970s, Peter Gillquist, a former Campus Crusade for Christ staffer, kicked a hornet's nest when, in his book *Love Is Now*,[71] he called for an end to this paranoia-producing practice. ("Why do you make trial of God by placing upon the neck of the disciples a yoke which neither we nor our fathers have been able to bear?" Acts 15:10) He had raised a very serious theological question that no one has ever wanted to face. If God has forgiven your sins, past, present, and future, when he shed his blood on the Cross, are they forgiven or not? This was already debated in the nineteenth century with a different focus, that of Universal Salvation: did Jesus merely *try* to save the human race, or did he *save* the human race? If the latter, everybody will go to heaven whether they repent or not. Well, neither Gillquist nor his critics were Universalists, but they debated a related issue: If, as they all held, God forgave your sins, past and future, in "the hour [you] first believed," why must a Christian continue to ask God's forgiveness, sin by sin? Hasn't that already been taken care of? "But don't I need forgiveness for sins I committed since my conversion?" I've got news for you: *all* your sins were in the future when Christ died for them, so there's no difference between sins past, present, and future as seen from your worm's eye perspective. Sure, if you slip up, you'll regret it and feel like kicking yourself, but the headband's not going to go off.

---

71. Peter E. Gillquist, *Love Is Now* (Grand Rapids: Zondervan, 1971), Chapter 4, "An Obsession with Confession," pp. 38–49.

Gillquist's opponents warned their audiences[72] not to heed him because if they relaxed and rejoiced in their easy freedom in Christ, they were laying on layer after layer of karmic cement. And here's where neurosis turns into flat-out superstition. Dare a Christian experiment with freedom from incessant confession? Maybe he should play it safe? Picture two guys walking down the street, one of them constantly snapping his fingers. Finally his friend can no longer ignore it and asks the inevitable question: "Uh, if you don't mind my asking, why all the finger-snapping?" The reply? "Oh, it's to keep the tigers away!" His buddy: "But there are no tigers around here!" His pal smiles and says, "See? It's working!"

Two Can Play This Game

In his brilliant book *The Psychology of Atheism*[73] Robert C. Sproul makes a case that it is *atheism*, not religion, that is the universal obsession of mankind. He brings the perspectives of Freud as well as Rudolf Otto[74] to bear on Romans 1:18: "Men by their wickedness suppress the truth." Paul, echoing contemporary Hellenistic synagogue preaching, claims that the problem of pagan Gentiles is not that they have sought

---

72. I remember hearing Lehman Strauss bemoaning the Gillquist heresy in a sermon given at Brookdale Baptist Church in Bloomfield, NJ.

73. Robert C. Sproul, *The Psychology of Atheism* (Minneapolis: Bethany Fellowship, 1974).

74. Rudolf Otto, *The Idea of the Holy: An Inquiry into the Non-Rational Factor in the Idea of the Divine and Its Relation to the Rational*. Trans. John W. Harvey (NY: Oxford University Press. 1924).

the true God but failed to find him, but that they *did* have an awareness of God and turned from it. They have suppressed this original knowledge of God to exchange it for *idolatry*, implicitly including polytheism. And from this apostasy stemmed the notorious immorality of pagan religion. Think of all the myths of the Greek gods raping mortal women! *That's* your moral paragon? No wonder so many Gentiles got disgusted with paganism and became "God fearers," attending synagogue though balking at full conversion to Judaism.

To borrow a term from D.Z. Phillips, Sproul has explored the "depth grammar" of Romans 1:18, expanding the scope of "idolatry" to cover secular self-worship or self-centeredness, a life-stance that is self-serving and convenient rather than self-threatening and costly like worshipping the Living God. *How* is an encounter with God threatening? Why would we want to turn away from it? Because God is *Wholly Other*. The encounter with the Holy is overwhelming not least because it reveals inescapably one's own pitiful finitude. "Woe is me!" Isaiah cries at the visionary encounter with Adonai (Isa. 6:5). Moses, having stumbled upon holy ground, falls prone and dares not look at God Revealed (Exod. 3:6–7). Peter, stunned at a miraculous catch of fish, bows at Jesus' feet, saying, "Depart from me, O Lord, for I am a sinful man!" (Luke 5:8–9). This, Otto proposed, was when and how particular religions began. Despite the holy terror, the revelation of the Deity simultaneously fascinates us, implicitly promising to fulfill our finitude with its infinity. It has, and *is*, what we lack: the Power of Being.

But not everyone turns to the offered embrace. For many (and here, taking Paul's direction, Sproul says this includes the entire human race), the trauma of the encounter with the Holy is *repressed*. One may retort, "Lord, when did we ever see you so?" (Matt. 25:39, 44). It happens early on, as we leave behind the child's innocence. The Eden story thus describes what happens in the case of every man and woman. For Freud, the universal trauma that gets buried in the subconscious is different; it is the child's chancing to catch the disturbing sight of his parents having sex. Sproul replaces this with an alarming encounter with the Divine Reality. This is what, he says, we have all repressed.

What Freud called "the return of the repressed" occurs in the form of a neurotic reaction, which comforts even though it is false. Our subconscious taps us on the shoulder via symbolic dreams, "Freudian" slips, psychosomatic illnesses, and dysfunctional, neurotic behaviors. We tend to ignore what these symptoms are trying to tell us (i.e., what we are trying to get ourselves to recognize): the original trauma. Therapy seeks to help us understand these signals and clues, because once the nature of the original trauma is revealed and dealt with, the neurotic behaviors should stop. But we have reached an accommodation with our misery, and we would rather suffer in silence than dare to face the core problem. C.S. Lewis depicts this in powerful story form in a scene in *The Great Divorce*[75] when an angel pleads with a soul to let him strike off a loathsome red reptile parasitically rooted into his shoulder. It represents some perversion that, by itself, sent the fellow to hell and keeps him there. Ironically, we fear the trauma that would deliver us from the trauma that occasioned the whole business!

What are the neurotic symptoms of the turning from God's mighty Presence in our lives? They include self-serving

---

75. C.S. Lewis, *The Great Divorce* (NY: Macmillan, 1946), pp. 98–102.

atheism, agnosticism, or liberal, nonthreatening religion. These things shield our awareness of our vulnerability before an all-seeing God, which is unbearable to the ungodly who would rather pretend God is not watching. See John 3:19–21; Gen. 2:25; 3:6–7; Psalm 139:1–4.

In sum, we feel shame and want to deny there is anyone to feel guilty before, whereas the healthy response would be to seek forgiveness, repentance, and restoration. We do not want to acknowledge God's sovereignty and would rather do our own thing, so we pretend there is no God. It would be healthy to yield and seek to conform our wills to the will of our creator which is thus the law/essence of our own being. Atheism is, then, an adolescent rebellion against just authority, the authority of the truth about ourselves and our lives no less than the truth about God. The "freedom" we seek is in fact slavery to our passions.

I doubt that we could really establish that each individual has had a traumatic encounter with the Numinous, but that is equally true of Freud's claim that every individual at some point beheld Mommy and Daddy getting it on. Both claims alike might be regarded as a deduction from a theory of Original Sin: "It *must* have happened!" Well, maybe.

In any case, I think playwright Paddy Chayefsky[76] gives us a perfect portrayal of a man suppressing the knowledge of God that once he had.

GIDEON. Oh, my Lord, let me go!

THE ANGEL. Let you go?

---

76. Paddy Chayefsky, *Gideon* (NY: Dramatists Play Service, 1961, 1962), pp. 64–68.

GIDEON. We have made a covenant of love between us, you and I. Release me from that covenant.

THE ANGEL. Are you suggesting some sort of divorce between your God and you?

GIDEON. We make an ill-matched pair, my Lord. You surely see we never meet but tempers rise between us. It is too much for me, this loving God. I cannot manage it. I am a plain man and subject to imperfect feelings. I shall betray you many times, and you shall rise in wrath against me and shall punish me with mighty penalties, and I cannot continue in this way, my Lord. Oh, let me say it plainly. I do not love you, Lord, and it is unreasonable to persist with each other when there is no love.

THE ANGEL. (*Startled.*) You do not love me?

GIDEON. (*Crosses to the Angel, kneels.*) I tried to love you, but it is too much for me. You are too vast a concept for me. To love you, God, one must be a god himself . . . I cannot love you, God, for it makes me a meaningless thing.

[. . .]

THE ANGEL. (*Crosses to Gideon.*) I meant you to love me, yet you are merely curious. You have no feeling for me then at all?

GIDEON. I fear you, God. I am in mortal dread of you. Perhaps that is the only love a man can give his god. [. . .] Let me go, God.

THE ANGEL. Let you go –whatever does that mean? Gideon, there is no divorce from God. (*Rises*) I am truth and exist. You cannot deny that I am. I stand palpably here before you, as real as rock, a very actual thing with whom you have commerced face-to-face.

GIDEON. Aye, my Lord. I see you and hear you. So I beg of you, my Lord—go from my sight. Make not your presence known to me again that I might say: "God is a dream, a name, a thought, but not a real thing."

THE ANGEL. But I am a real thing.

GIDEON. I would pretend that you were not. (*The Angel is a little startled at this.*)

THE ANGEL. Let me review this. You would pretend God is not although you know that he is, so that you might be a significant creature which you know you are not.

[...]

GIDEON. My Lord?

THE ANGEL. Yes? (*Gideon looks around the stage.*)

GIDEON. God?

THE ANGEL. Here, Gideon, by the press.

GIDEON. Are you still here?

THE ANGEL. Here, over here.

GIDEON. (*Standing.*) Ah, yes, you do seem blurred. (*Crosses to the Angel*) My Lord, I asked you for one small thing, that I might delude myself with some spurious grandeur.

THE ANGEL. And I answered: "No, it will not do." You want the universe to please your eye, Gideon, and not mine. You would be God yourself. Hear me well, O Hebrew. I am a jealous God and brook no other gods, not even you. Why have I come here at all but to put an end to false idols? You have done well in pulling down the effigies of Ba-al, but do not think to set yourself up on their empty altars. Do not make a cult of man, not even in fancy.

GIDEON. (*Looking around.*) My Lord? My Lord?

THE ANGEL. Attend me, Gideon, and mark my words.

GIDEON. My Lord?

THE ANGEL. Where are you looking, Gideon? I am here.

GIDEON. My Lord, where are you gone?

THE ANGEL. Here! I stand here, by the wine-press here! I have not moved!

GIDEON. My Lord, please speak to me. We are not finished.

THE ANGEL. What is this game?

GIDEON. My Lord!

THE ANGEL. I stand right here!

GIDEON. Where are you, Lord? The matter is not finished!

THE ANGEL. (*Crying out.*) O Gideon, do not forsake me!

GIDEON. God! Where are you, God?

Here is Sproul's scenario exactly: the crushing burden of the Divine Presence, the nullity of the human standing before it, the willful shirking of the theophany, the suppression of the inner voice of God.

Sproul's argument does not debunk atheism. Inevitably,

you're going to have to default to philosophical arguments for and against God's existence, not our business here. *If* there is a God, Sproul may be right. If there *isn't*, Freud may be right. But that does not render Sproul's thinking worthless or irrelevant. Indeed, I think he has well described what happens to many who rebel, not necessarily against a really existing deity, but against a *belief* in one. Religion has been oppressive to them, and they finally cast off the yoke of it. But religion did have deep roots in them, and it festers there once the one-time believer thinks to have dug it out. There may in that case be neurotic symptoms such as Sproul describes, perhaps most notably a fanatical hatred for religion. Such a person

> is still reacting unconsciously . . ., and it is as if he had an unconscious belief in a supernatural God of the sort he rejects consciously. His battle against this unconscious belief in a supernatural God is represented in his belief system by the "crying need . . . to free [his] fellow men from the deadening shackles of superficiality of belief, creedalism, and supernaturalism."[77]

Galatians 1:23 says of Paul, "He who once persecuted us is now preaching the faith he once tried to destroy." But it is exactly reversed in the case of the one whom Max Scheler calls "the apostate."

> An "apostate" is not a man who once in his life radically changes his deepest religious, political, legal, or philosophical convictions—even when this change is not continuous, but involves a certain rupture. Even after his conversion, the true "apostate" is not primarily committed to the positive

---

77. Helfaer, *Psychology of Religious Doubt*, p. 259.

contents of his new belief and to the realization of its aims. He is motivated by the struggle against the old belief and lives only for its negation. The apostate does not affirm his new convictions for their own sake, he is engaged in a continuous chain of acts of revenge against his own spiritual past. In reality he remains a captive of this past, and the new faith is merely a handy frame of reference for negating and rejecting the old. As a religious type, the apostate is therefore at the opposite pole from the "resurrected," whose life is transformed by a new faith which is full of intrinsic meaning and values.[78]

Militant, crusading atheism, with its scorched-earth campaigns to suppress and outlaw public expressions of religious faith, would seem to be the perfect example of what Scheler describes: absolute negation. Is there an atheist gospel? Or must we conclude that, for them, "no news is good news"? The vengeful God-hater has rewritten Galatians 1:23: "He who once belonged to us is now trying to destroy the faith he once preached." Maybe these crusaders are right and there is no God. I agree with them, but I have found greater peace by taking people as they come and accepting that their beliefs are not my business. So I am not saying atheism *per se* is superstition any more than religion is. But superstition and neurosis can be found in both. Not too surprisingly, some individuals have found existential relief by converting *to* faith, while others have found peace by converting *from* it.[79]

---

78. Max Scheler, *Ressentiment*. Trans. Lewis B. Coser and William W. Holdheim (Milwaukee: Marquette University Press, 1994), pp. 47–48.

79. Helfaer, *Psychology of Religious Doubt*.

Chapter Five

Charis-magic

Television preachers have come in for their fair share of ridicule and criticism, much of it because of their moral hypocrisy or their use of the "ministry" as a way of ministering to their own bank accounts.[80] While these media evangelists have earned every bit of ridicule they have received, there is a more serious criticism, one that must still apply if none of them were hypocrites and hucksters. Their brand of Christianity constitutes a backsliding even from traditional fundamentalism, a devolution from religion, however simpleminded, to magic pure and simple. If the televised antics of Peter Popov, Benny Hinn, and Jimmy Swaggart have ever reminded the reader of those of a prancing witchdoctor, this is no accident. On the fringes of the contemporary Pentecostal and Charismatic movements we are witnessing a retreat from religion to sorcery.

---

80. James Randi, *The Faith Healers* (Buffalo: Prometheus Books, 1987), especially chapters 4, 8, 9.

Here I will be utilizing the classic definition of magic proposed by Sir James Frazer (*The Golden Bough*). This pioneer (albeit armchair) anthropologist theorized that humanity's first ritual dealings with the supernatural were strictly businesslike. The suppliant performed the requisite sacrifice or chant, and the god (or demon or *deva* or ancestor) was obliged to "come through" with the desired blessing, usually a material one. One must indeed beware of the numinous power which might resent its binding and use by puny humans, lashing out if one were not careful. But this was not what we should consider real worship. One had to avoid offending the god, but there was no thought that immoral conduct might offend him. It was pure business, though potentially dangerous business, rather like dealing with the Mob. The believer in magic did not bother to purify his heart before going up to the Temple of the Lord; he merely made sure he carried with him a long spoon to dine with the devil.

What distinguishes magic from religion is that the former is simply a matter of the manipulation of supernatural power for selfish ends, and involves no real element of either adoration or morality. Frazer felt that these elements belonged only to a later stage of social development, that of religious faith. He believed that religion had evolved from magic. Magic was a pseudo-science by which early people thought they could manipulate (super)natural laws, just as science manipulates gravity, magnetism, etc. One such supernatural law is that of sympathy, i.e., that one of two paired items can be used to influence the other. *Imitative magic* presupposed that something done to a representation of a thing causes the same harm or blessing to befall the thing imitated. The best-known example would be a Voodoo doll.

Contagious magic assumes that if two things have previously been in contact, something done to one thing will happen to the other. For example, gathering nail clippings for hexes on the person they used to belong to.

Frazer reasoned that people eventually must have wised up and realized that this magical pseudo-science was unreliable, hit-or-miss, which it simply couldn't be if it were a matter of manipulating reliable laws. So they came up with an alternative theory of what was going on, one that would factor in an uncertainty principle. This was *religion*, in which you were not manipulating *laws* or commanding demons, but rather making requests of *personal wills*. The whims or the better judgments of the gods might cause them to turn down your request this time. But that didn't mean you were barking up the wrong tree. Better luck next time!

Granted, there were problems with Frazer's theory. For one thing, people often seem oblivious of the empirical failure of beliefs they cherish, so they probably never would have given up magic in the first place. For another, are magic and religion really that different? Some magic (e.g., the rituals of the Order of the Golden Dawn) seems essentially religious, while the rituals of religion (e.g., Catholic Mass, Vedic sacrifice) have an element of manipulation of the divine. When the priest consecrates the host, it does and must become the body of Christ; you don't just hope it works this week. But this criticism does not seem fatal to Frazer's model. We just have to remember that lived reality seldom neatly conforms to the theoretical categories we like to use in order to analyze it. You set up, in this case, two "ideal types," textbook definitions. Then you use them as yardsticks to measure the inevitably sloppier phenomena. No one possesses a time travel machine, so we'll never know for sure whether (or why or how) religion actually did evolve from magic. The important thing, I think, is the typological value of the categories. They make it possible for us to say, "This practice is closer to magic; that one is closer to religious faith." So I will adopt these categories as conceptual tools for the present analysis.

Are there magical elements in the Charismatic-Pentecostal movement today? Indeed, there seem to be. And though they are most obviously to be found in rather extreme elements of the movement, they are not restricted to the fringes, and their implications are wider still. At any rate, the most obvious practice of "charis-magic" occurs in the "prosperity gospel" circles of Kenneth Copeland, Jim Bakker, Joel Osteen, and elements of the Full Gospel Businessmen's Fellowship International. On the basis of various sections of scripture, leaders in this movement insist that God wants his children, the "King's kids,"[81] to live it up! One of the main sources of this message seems to be certain alleged "promises" of God which the believer is to appropriate. Here we can see magical bargaining pure and simple. The magician wants material benefits and intends to get them. Norvell Hayes shamelessly advises women to ask God for closets full of new clothes.[82] Kenneth Hagin exhorts hearers to have "Cadillac faith," since only those of little faith will be satisfied with a Buick.[83]

The supplicant won't take "no" for an answer. One often

81. See Harold Hill, *Instant Answers for King's Kids in Training* (Plainfield, New Jersey: Logos International, 1978).

82. Sermon attended by this writer in Montclair, New Jersey, 1978.

83. Kenneth Hagin, "Practicing Faith" (Los Angeles: Full Gospel Businessmen's Fellowship (audiotape).

hears the confident affirmation: "I *demand* so-and-so from God!" While this passes for simply a strengthened version of the pious idiom "claiming the promises," it thinly veils the speaker's claim to have bound God's power like that of a familiar spirit. One almost expects to hear "I say 'jump!' and God says 'How high?'!" And how does the pray-er dare to push God around in this manner? Of course, he is only claiming those scriptural promises. The favorites are Mark 11:24, "I tell you, then, whatever you ask for in prayer, believe that you have received it and it will be yours," and 3 John 2, "I pray that you may prosper even as your soul prospers." It means nothing to the charismagus that these texts are taken out of context; they are simply incantatory formulae, power-words that pulse with occult energy simply by virtue of their presence in a magic book.

While the preternatural powers of charis-magic are purportedly available to all, it is not surprising that certain adepts hold center stage. In Asia, Africa, and South America, they are called *shamans*, better known to Westerners as "witch-doctors" or "medicine-men." The Charismatic movement has no dearth of them. I will briefly review five shamanistic traits shared conspicuously by the Pentecostal practitioners.[84]

---

84. The two terms "Pentecostal" and "Charismatic" may be used as nearly synonymous, the main difference being primarily historical. "Pentecostal" refers to the many glossolalic, prophetic, and faith healing denominations formed early in the twentieth century by fundamentalists who had abandoned (or been kicked out of) the staid "establishment" denominations like the Baptists, Presbyterians, and Methodists. Pentecostal denominations include the Assemblies of God, Church of God (Cleveland, Tennessee), Church of God in Christ, Church of God of Prophecy, Pentecostal Holiness, and Pentecostal Free Will Baptists. "Charismatic" refers to a movement, started in

First, the shaman receives both his vocation and his powers by virtue of a visionary journey to the world of spirits/ancestors. This experience may even be conceived of as a temporary death. Most of the charismagicians have had similar "calling" experiences, since the role of such visions in prophetic and millenarian religion is well known. But it is worth mentioning that Kenneth Hagin, for instance, put great stock in a series of personal visions, starting with a youthful deathbed experience of descending three times into hell.[85] Here we have a remarkably close parallel to the shamanistic journey to the realm of the dead.

Second, the shaman is equipped for his task with a clothing of elemental power, known generically as "*mana*." This *mana* is roughly equivalent to "the Force" in *Star Wars*. Though any individual may accumulate *mana* (and so good fortune and prosperity), the shaman is endowed with it to a singular degree. He radiates the life-force. Kenneth Hagin would present himself as eradicating disease virtually by his mere presence. Travelling with a diabetic friend, "I told him, 'You won't register any sugar as long as you're with me!'"[86] Or think of the endless offers of "healing handkerchiefs," or appeals to "put your hand on the radio." Oral Roberts used to defend these phenomena

---

the late 1960s and blossoming in the 70s, within the mainline denominations and the Roman Catholic Church, but with the same theology and spiritual manifestations as the classical Pentecostals. Charismatics chose to (and were allowed to) remain within their original churches. People from both groups often attend the same nondenominational retreats, revivals, rallies, and parachurch organizations.

85. Hagin, *I Believe in Visions*, pp. 9ff.

86. Kenneth Hagin, *Authority of the Believer* (Tulsa: Kenneth Hagin Evangelistic Association, 1975), p. 29.

as mere psychological "points of contact," but it is clear what impression is given the believer; the *mana* possessed by the healer is so great that it attaches even to material objects he has personally touched (or broadcast his voice through!).

Third, the medicine-man is endowed with specific abilities to serve the community. Prominent among them is rain-making, or the ability to control weather. It is quite common to hear evangelicals try to control the elements via prayer ("Lord, give us a good day for this rally."). But the claims of the Charismatic leaders can go way beyond this. Franklin Hall writes of past victories, how "five times the author commanded it to stop raining during the time people came to services in the evening. On May 20 [for example], within five minutes the heavens quit raining as commanded. . . . In nearly every city we come to we find it necessary to do something about the elements. If it is too cold, we command the temperature to rise. If it is too hot, the temperature must come down."[87] A hagiographic booklet collecting some miracles of faith-healer William Branham recounts how "In Germany he confounded the witch doctors who came out in force to frustrate his ministry. They actually succeeded in bringing a huge black cloud over the tent which with tornadic force would rip it to shreds. Brother Branham stepped on the platform and in Jesus' Name the cloud was instantly dispersed and the sun shone through."[88]

Fourth, the shaman can send hexes and curses on his

87. Franklin Hall, *Subduing the Earth, Controlling the Elements and Ruling the Nations with Jesus Christ* (Franklin Hall, 1966), p. 43.

88. *Twentieth Century Prophet, The Messenger to the Laodicean Church Age* (Jeffersonville, IN: Spoken Word Publications, n.d.), p. 43.

enemies. We are not far from such voodoo when Hagin claims "You can actually exercise authority over others as long as they are in your presence.... When folks in my family get excessively angry, I just take authority over it. They know when I do because they look at me with a startled expression."[89] More obviously punitive measures include the abrupt silencing of an antiglossolalic speaker by a "Full Gospel pastor" of Hagin's acquaintance.[90] Similarly, Franklin Hall recounts the destruction by tornado of a town which had rejected his preaching of his "gravity-free Christalujah Power" and the "Fire-and-cloud space flight ministry."[91] Another illustration comes to us from the venerable pages of *TV Guide.* There born-again musical celebrity Pat Boone describes how he sought to stop his daughter's backsliding by tacking up a picture of Jesus among the rock star posters in her room. Then he walked around the room "binding the demons." One may wonder if he had a headdress and a feathered rattle with him.

A garage mechanic made the mistake of ridiculing William Branham, and "Before he could get to his own garage, his own son-in-law, backing out of the door with his truck full of scrap iron, struck him, crushing both his feet and ankles." An irate woman, as she was leaving a Branham meeting, "stumbled over a board, and falling to the ground, she broke her arm in fifteen places." Recalling those who made excuses not to attend the Great Supper, one man rebuffed Branham's invitation to attend a revival: "'We are too busy to go to any revival; we raise

---

89. Hagin, *Authority of the Believer*, p. 30.

90. Hagin, *Authority of the Believer*, p. 31.

91. This nomenclature, which would seem downright glossolalic, is "explained" in Hall's astonishing *Miracle Word Magazine*, Spring 1979.

chickens and haven't time for anything like that.' However, shortly after that, this man died, so he didn't raise any more chickens."[92] *Schadenfreude*? I'd say so. Superstition? You bet.

Fifth, the shaman is the intermediary between mortals and the supernatural realm. His intercession with gods is necessarily more effective than ordinary prayers. And along the same lines, Rex Humbard would invite his viewers to mail in their prayer requests for him to take to the foot of the Cross itself in Jerusalem. Oral Roberts would do the same at his Oklahoma "Prayer Tower." In each case the implicit claim is that the shaman's prayers have a greater chance of compelling an otherwise reluctant divinity to act, and all the more so as he takes the prayer requests to the sacred "axis mundi" (Golgotha or the Prayer Tower) linking heaven and earth.[93] Here is the portal through which prayers may ascend before the gods. This is, I believe, no mere analogy.

I have been concentrating on the leaders of the Pentecostal fringe, but much of the same superstitious framework is relevant to their many adherents. They, too, are told to partake of the various occult powers, though one suspects that the leaders function vicariously in this respect. That is, most of their fans never personally experience such spectacles, but their faith is buttressed by the fact that at least *someone* does. You see the same thing in the kindred circles of the Prosperity Gospel. These Cadillac-driving preachers tell you that you, too, can become wealthy by claiming prosperity from the Divine Source. But how many do? It is like buying a lottery ticket when

92. *Twentieth Century Prophet,* pp. 46–47.

93. See Mircea Eliade's discussion of "sacred space" in *The Sacred and the Profane: The Nature of Religion.* Trans. Willard R. Trask (NY: Harcourt, Brace & World, Inc., 1959), pp. 20ff.

you hear that someone else in your neighborhood won the Big Prize. There's at least *some* chance that lightning will strike twice, right? As long as the shaman himself performs miracles, then the believer's faith in the miraculous is confirmed.

In my comparison of extremist Pentecostalism with classical magic, I hope to have made certain puzzling aspects of the movement more understandable. And all of it taken together should help explain one more interesting fact. Why is it that fringe Pentecostalism has to deal seriously with admitted magic and "witchcraft" in its own ranks, especially in inner-city areas? The answer is that it is a family argument. The two are close enough to throw stones. Suburban Assemblies of God believers may disdain black magic or palmistry as a theoretical pitfall from which they hope to see "hippies" and others converted. But the fringe Pentecostals must actively fight against adherence to pagan witchcraft in their own midst.[94] James Rector chides "superstitious saints" with these words: "Some Church Folks are so Superstitious that they won't walk under a ladder. . . . They wear Root Bags, and Rabbit's Feet." But "if they had the HOLY GHOST in their Life, they would not be Afraid or SUPERSTITIOUS!"[95] But one does not wonder that such beliefs would tempt the followers of Reverend Rector who goes on to tell of his experiences with "The Snake Woman,"

---

94. One informant, a member of R. W. Shambach's Miracle Temple in Newark, New Jersey, speaks of constant accusations and admissions of "witchcraft" among the members. These charges may be confirmed by means such as seeing ectoplasmic snakes hovering over the heads of the culprits!

95. James Rector, *Demons, Witches and Warlocks* (Cincinnati: The United Christian Fellowship of America, n.d.), p. 6. [Rector's capitalization and grammar.]

"The Spider Woman," and "The Demon on the Bridge"![96] This minister fulminates against "root-bags" and amulets, but distributes blessed crosses and vials of anointing oil. In effect, his message is "Your superstition is false, but my superstition is true!" One is the mirror image of the other, and it is easy for fringe Pentecostals to step "through the looking glass."

---

96. Rector, *Demons, Witches and Warlocks*, p. 9.

Chapter Six

Devil's Advocates

I should think that the most extreme case of reducing Christianity to abject superstition must be the Pentecostal/ Charismatic "Deliverance Ministry," led by Don Basham, Frank and Ida Mae Hammond, and Pat Brooks. These people think to exorcize literally demonic influences that have taken root even in Born-Again Christians, hitherto thought to be immune. There are no symptoms such as those showcased in William Peter Blatty's *The Exorcist*, like spewing green bile, a possessed person floating in the air above her urine-stained mattress, barking out obscenities in foreign languages one has never learned, etc. No indeed. Instead, for the Deliverance Ministry, the results of "demonization" are familiar and mundane "besetting sins" of which the frustrated Christian just cannot seem to repent.

Incidentally, why the term "demonization" rather than the usual "demon possession"? "Demonization" is strictly more accurate as a translation of the Greek *daimonazo*. But one also suspects that such lexical discrimination is intended to avoid the main objection offered by non-Deliverance evangelicals, namely that, since Born-Again Christians are indwelt by God's Holy Spirit, they cannot possibly be sheltering unclean spirits at the same time. "What fellowship hath Christ with Belial?" (2 Cor. 6:15). Of course, these pious Christians do not deny that Satan and his team constantly pelt them with sundry temptations, but they cannot harm one so long as the believer dons "the whole armor of God" (Eph. 6:11). Jesus, after all, could be (and was) tempted by the devil, but he certainly was not (and could not have been) demon-possessed. Apparently, "demonization" falls somewhere between temptation and possession. But, really, it would seem to be a "difference without a distinction" in view of the methods employed to cast out the demonic affliction. It is exorcism. Exorcism of regenerate Christians, even though that is supposed to be impossible—so let's call it something else: "deliverance."

What rain produced this growth of theological toadstools? The felt need for demon-deliverance is the result of the failure of traditional techniques of sanctification. Many evangelicals and fundamentalists embrace a gradualist approach to spiritual and moral growth. This amounts to daily "appropriation" of Christ's transformative power. One reluctantly expects frequent setbacks and failures, but one expects a gradual increase in holiness. Others teach a "second blessing" theology whereby the initial experience of being born again and receiving the Holy Spirit is, or should be, followed by an experience of the Spirit occasioned by an entire surrender to God's will and Christ's Lordship. This Second Blessing, or Baptism with the Spirit, ostensibly produces a Deeper Life or Victorious Christian Life plus greater power for Christian service, especially new courage for personal witnessing. The Second Blessing is, in short, a jump-start in the process of Sanctification. But sooner or later it turns out to be as big a disappointment as the First Blessing. In effect, "deliverance" becomes a "Third Blessing," and of course it's not going to work either.

The situation is exactly analogous to that obtaining in the case of divine healing. Pentecostals, like New Thought and Christian Science believers, believe in a "healing" version of the Second Blessing: since 1 Peter 2:24 says, "by his stripes [i.e., lash-wounds, metonymy for the cross] we are healed," physical healing must be available by means of the "mind game" of "appropriation," healing by faith. But of course this does not work most of the time. When it does not, there is a stand-by fall-back position: blame the victim. You *thought* you had the needed faith for the healing, but you must not have. Better luck next time! You may eventually quietly despair and resign yourself not only to your continuing ailments but also to a burden of guilt for your lack of faith. But wait—maybe there is one more thing to try. Suppose you *have* been healed, but Satan is hiding it from you, "counterfeiting the symptoms," as one often hears in these circles. So what do you do about it? "Rebuke" Satan and/or his phantom pains! Watchman Nee used to do this.

> If God's Word is truth, I thought, then what are these symptoms? They all must be lies! So I declared to the enemy, "This sleeplessness is a lie, this headache is a lie, this fever is a lie, this high pulse is a lie. In view of what God has said to me, all these symptoms of sickness are just your lies. . . ." In

five minutes I was asleep, and I awoke the following morning feeling perfectly well.[97]

Pentecostalism began when some Holiness believers felt the need for a definite crisis experience that would enable the seeker to know when/that he or she had received the Spirit-baptism. They decided that the definitive "sign" was glossolalia, speaking in tongues.[98] The "corroborating crisis" for the healing movement was obvious: if you received the prayed-for healing, or thought you did, the physical relief would itself serve as the authenticating "sign." But how about the Deliverance Ministry? What could convince you that the demons were gone? The "sign" for the Deliverance Ministry is, ah, *vomiting* up the demons. Pretty traumatic, perhaps theatrical enough to make you believe a major turning point has been reached. This could work, as anthropologist Claude Lévi-Strauss shows in his essay, "The Effectiveness of Symbols."[99] There he recounts a shamanic ritual in which an African medicine-man enables a pregnant woman to give birth to a child who has kept her waiting too long. In his chant the shaman summons various mythical and folklore beings, enlisting them in the unseen struggle with the forces holding back the delivery. Lévi-Strauss theorizes that

---

97. Nee, *Normal Christian Life*, p. 76.

98. Donald W. Dayton, *Theological Roots of Pentecostalism* (Grand Rapids: Francis Asbury Press/Zondervan, 1987); Walter J. Hollenweger, *The Pentecostals* (Peabody: Hendrickson Publishers, 1988); John L. Sherrill, *They Speak with other Tongues*. Spire Books (Old Tappan: Fleming H. Revell, 1965).

99. Claude Lévi-Strauss, *Structural Anthropology*. Trans. Claire Jacobson and Brooke Grundfest Schoepf (Garden City: Doubleday Anchor Books, 1967), Chapter X, "The Effectiveness of Symbols," pp. 181–201.

the "magic" of the rite is the "handle" it gives the woman to gain control over a problem whose mysterious vagueness had baffled and amazed her.

But the belief in intractable "counterfeit" symptoms and in demons who can be cast out for a while, only to return with seven of their drinking buddies (Matt. 12:43–45) is really an exercise in *theodicy*, attempting to get God off the hook for reneging on his (supposed) promises. If God promised sanctification, miraculous healing, and deliverance from demons, but there were no lasting results, is he not at fault? God forbid! The pious Christian cannot afford to believe that, or, logically, he would have to doubt the Big Promise: that faith in Christ will bring salvation. So, as the cliché goes, "It's not you, it's me." Isn't that just the point of Romans 3:4? "Let God be true though every man be false, as it is written, 'That thou mayest be justified in thy words, and prevail when thou art judged.'"

In the same vein, it is rather unsettling to see the ease with which evangelical missionaries assimilate the animistic paganism encountered in the field into the categories of their own belief. They do not doubt the reality of the tribal god N'kangu; they merely preach that their god Jesus is stronger, able to protect converts with greater spirit-power. Domestically, one can notice an equivalent phenomenon in the late-night gatherings of fundamentalist young people, trading secondhand stories of demon-possession. Though of course they believe in the factuality of these hair-raising reports (compiled for instance in *Demon Experiences in Many Lands*),[100] the scene is much the same as the old game of swapping ghost-stories around the campfire. When one

---

100. *Demon Experiences in Many Lands: a Compilation* (Chicago: Moody Press, 1972).

person piously terminates the session, saying "Listen, we're really glorifying Satan by talking about him like this; let's talk about the Lord instead," the meaning in plain English is: "Hey, no more ghost stories! I'm too scared to walk back to my tent as it is!"

Beelzebultmann?

There is another, far more important, theological question implied in all this, namely, the question preliminary to the much-debated problem of "demythologizing," the translation of the self-understanding of the New Testament Christians into modern, non-supernatural categories. In his famous essay "New Testament and Mythology,"[101] Rudolf Bultmann contended that "modern man" is far from holding to the worldview of the New Testament, with its supernatural entities and interventions. Evangelical apologists have, predictably, rejected the allegation. After all, *they* certainly inhabit the twenty-first century *and* accept supernaturalism. But they miss Bultmann's point. He meant that no one today really *lives* as though he believed in the miraculous world of the New Testament, and actions speak louder than words. But to this rule the Deliverance Ministry forms a notable exception: if *anyone* goes the full Monty when it comes to New Testament supernaturalism, it's the Deliverance Ministry. I won't go so far as to accuse Basham, the Hammonds and the rest of "the hobgoblin consistency of little minds." No, but they are certainly consistent about hobgoblins.

101. Rudolf Bultmann, "New Testament and Mythology" in *Kerygma and Myth: A Theological Debate*. Hans Werner Bartsch, ed. Harper Torchbooks (NY: Harper & Row, 1961), pp. 1–44.

Just what is the New Testament view of demon activity? What does demon-possession (or "demonization") mean? This condition might manifest itself in the forms of frenzy (Mark 9:18), supernatural knowledge (Mark 1:24), superhuman strength (Luke 8:29), common illness or handicap (Luke 13:11), or various combinations of these symptoms. Most "Bible-believers" would claim to believe that nothing has changed since New Testament days. Yet there is in fact a curious limitation in their picture of demon activity. While the gospels regard demon activity as a common cause of serious illness, as most prescientific societies do,[102] modern evangelicals by and large do not. Instead, they picture demonization almost exclusively in terms of fits of blasphemous frenzy a la *The Exorcist*. And instead of the commonplace occurrence of demon affliction we see in the gospels, most evangelicals expect it to occur only among foreign pagans or occultists in California. In the synoptic gospels it seems like Jesus is thronged by ailing demoniacs on every street corner. But when a middleclass suburban Baptist gets arthritis or pneumonia, will it even occur to him or her to call in an exorcist? No, for them, demon possession is the stuff of missionary ghost stories but, thankfully, do not form part of the world they live in.

When was the last time you offered your condolences to a neighbor whose son is demon-possessed? Demons are just not encountered in everyday life, contrary to what one would expect if the New Testament worldview still held good.

---

102. I.M. Lewis, *Ecstatic Religion: An Anthropological Study of Spirit Possession and Shamanism*. Pelican Anthropology Library (Baltimore: Penguin, 1971); Victor Turner, *The Drums of Affliction: A Study of Religious Processes among the Ndembu of Zambia*. Symbol, Myth and Ritual Series (Ithaca: Cornell University Press, 1981).

With Deliverance believers, on the other hand, the picture is altogether different. They are ready to attribute almost any serious problem or sickness at least potentially to demons. (See the amazing list of demon-symptoms in the Hammond's *Pigs in the Parlor.*[103]) The remedy is exorcism, even self-exorcism. The reality of the demonic is once again encountered in everyday life, in the form of sickness, not just frenzy, and here at home, not just in far-flung mission-fields. Will the real upholder of the New Testament worldview please stand up?

The seriousness of the question thus posed should not be missed. Evangelicals and mainstream Pentecostals do not have much trouble in recognizing fanaticism when they see it in the Deliverance Ministry. Yet it seems to be the latter who adhere more closely to the biblical world-picture. And of course this case is only one of several degrees on a scale. Mainstream evangelicals have traditionally written off all Pentecostals and Charismatics as fanatics because of their practice of glossolalia and prophecy. But the strained rationalizations of the Dispensationalists could not mask the fact that it was Pentecostalism that was closer to the New Testament picture.

But moving it over another notch, Christians of a more theologically liberal ("Modernist") bent can be found snickering at the evangelical-fundamentalist belief in "the Rapture," a notion uncomfortably close to that of UFO cultists who expect to get "beamed up" en masse to the Mother Ship in the Last Days. In all these cases, the criterion seems to be the same. Basically each group stops short of the next because of its greater or lesser grip on everyday reality as most people experience it. To venture very far away from "normal" reality

---

103. Frank and Ida Mae Hammond, *Pigs in the Parlor: A Practical Guide to Deliverance* (Kirkwood, OH: Impact Books, 1973).

seems "fanatical," and some venture farther than others. The difference between the Deliverance Ministry and mainstream Evangelicalism-Pentecostalism raises (or should raise) Bultmann's question with acute clarity. Even to Pentecostal believers, Bultmann's charge has force: do you really believe in the New Testament picture of reality? And if you want to be consistent, which path will you follow--Deliverance, or demythologizing?

The examination of the Deliverance Ministry reveals it to be more than the internecine squabble it is often taken to be. Instead it raises questions crucial to the integrity of Evangelical-Pentecostal religion. Do believers really adhere to the New Testament worldview, as they claim, or are they ready to admit with Liberals that New Testament supernaturalism must be modified? And what about the perfectionism so common to Pentecostal- Charismatic spirituality? Are its promises realistic, or mustn't something be amiss if believers must fall back on a series of "fail-safe" maneuvers culminating in the Deliverance Ministry? And remember, prescientific belief turns into superstition once the scientific outlook becomes available.

Chapter Seven

Divination

There is in the everyday lives of fringe Charismatics (and some not so fringe) quite a dose of the primitive. The worldview inculcated by much popular Charismatic teaching and literature is essentially magical. For instance, Merlin Carothers teaches about a world wherein quite literally every piece of soggy toast, every stolen parking space, every headache is a sign from God to the believer.[104] This kind of worldview is aptly described (with reference to actual cultural primitives) by anthropologist Mary Douglas:

> The cosmos is turned in, as it were, on man. Its transforming energy is threaded onto the lives of individuals so that nothing happens in the way of storms, sickness, blights

104. Merlin Carothers, *Prison to Praise* (Plainfield, New Jersey: Logos International, 1971), p. 66; and *Bringing Heaven into Hell* (Old Tappan: New Jersey: Fleming H. Revell Company, 1976), p. 90.

or droughts except in virtue of these personal links. So the universe is man-centered in the sense that it must be interpreted in reference to humans.[105]

And how is such "interpretation" practiced in the world of Carothers? There are two ways. First, with Bill Gothard and almost all other fundamentalists, he suggests one examine apparently fortuitous events to divine the will of God. What is he trying to tell me?[106] In another culture, the believer might read the flight of geese or the entrails of chickens, but charismagician Merlin and his brethren advise us to read flat tires and collapsing chairs. And, secondly, if the divinely prescribed situation is a really dire one (illness, financial straits, etc.) one may avert divine pressure by the device of formulary "praise." The clear tendency of the anecdotes given by Carothers is to lead his readers to believe that if one praises God for the trials, God will relent. The stated rationale is that God will then have seen that the believer has learned his lesson of humble submission, and will call off the calamities. It is impossible to miss the plainly magical character of the whole schema. It is as if one manipulates, even outwits, the plaguing divinity by the requisite magic words, "Oh, praise you Lord for this cancer!" Brer Rabbit had the same idea when he begged to be thrown into the briar patch.

Second, there is a series of steps to follow in order to discern the will of God. When it is completed, you may move ahead "in the center of God's will." First, one "prays on it,"

---

105. Mary Douglas, "Primitive Thought-Worlds," in Roland Robertson (ed.), *Sociology of Religion* (Baltimore: Penguin Books, 1969), pp. 79–99.

106. Bill Gothard, *Institute in Basic Youth Conflicts* syllabus (LaGrange, IL: Institute in Basic Youth Conflicts, n.d.), n.p.

preferably several times, asking God to communicate his will, to be discerned by "feeling led." Then one tries to find relevant biblical verses (something that would seem to obviate the rest of the process), After that, one seeks the advice of fellow believers (again, a common-sense step that hardly requires all the pious rhetoric). You might also try "putting a fleece before the Lord" as Gideon did (Judg. 6:36–40), asking for some improbable "sign," though it is risky, as it might be construed as "putting God to the test." One supposes that just going through the steps shows you have done your best, allowing you to feel free to go ahead with your preferred course.

But what if the thing blows up in your face? You'd have to conclude you had done something wrong, made some mistake somewhere along the line. After a few such screw-ups, you might, like the ancient magician, decide that the whole approach should be dropped. "I don't know what God's truth is. . . . Do any of us?"[107] But fundamentalist piety has inculcated much anxiety in its flock, making them fear disastrous consequences if one "steps outside the will of God." Afraid of missing God's will, one will go through the same procedure next time, fully confident of finding God's will. If it fails again, you'll just shrug it off and repeat the pattern. The saying goes that if you keep doing the same thing hoping for a different result next time, that's the definition of insanity. Maybe so, but I'd be more inclined to say it's the definition of superstition.

And let's not forget about "cutting scripture," opening the Bible at random and letting one's eyes fall anywhere on the page, then trying to interpret the verse, regardless of context, as containing some clue about what you should do. This is in

---

107. Brian Moore, *Catholics* (NY: Paperback Library, 1973), p. 59.

effect a Christian version of the Chinese oracular system of the *I Ching*. Many fundamentalists flinch at the overtly superstitious character of the whole thing, but it is still frequently practiced. "Cutting scripture" has generated a widely circulating joke, a cautionary tale of sorts. A guy opens his Bible and spots the verse, "Judas went out and hanged himself" (Matt. 27:5). Yikes! So he quickly rifles though the India paper pages and stabs with his finger on a new verse: "Go thou and do likewise" (Luke10:37). Ulp! Third time's the charm, right? But this time he opens to "What thou doest, do quickly" (John 13:27).

The Bible as a Magic Book

For many years I have studied the theology underlying biblicism, the fundamentalist belief in the absolute authority of the Bible in every aspect of life, only to conclude that it is not theological in nature at all, but rather entirely psychological. That is, biblicism is not, as its adherents claim and think, an implication of a set of beliefs about the Bible but rather the outgrowth of a particular frame of mind. I am not impatient with theological claims; I just do not think they are the real source or motivation of biblicism, and this becomes evident once we discover certain inconsistencies in biblicism which make nonsense of its theological claims but are quite consistent with the psychological function of biblicism. If it were a matter of theology, surely biblicists would notice the problems. But since biblicism does the job biblicists want it to do, they simply never notice the problems.

Biblicism, again, is the term for that stance toward the Bible whereby a believer intends to obey whatever the text tells him to do, and to believe whatever the text asserts. If occasionally the commands of the Bible (say, to give away all one's possessions) seem just too outrageous, biblicists may rationalize them away, but even this does not mean they are not taking them seriously; a non-biblicist would say he rejects the command of the Bible and leave it at that. And there are more liberal Christian theologies which do not entail biblicism, managing, as Reinhold Niebuhr said, to take the text seriously even if not literally. So what is it that attracts many people to biblicism?

Faith as Skepticism

First I think we may identify the fundamentalist's, the biblicist's, desperate felt need for "a sure word from God." Why do we need God to break the silence of the ages with a revealed word, an inspired book of infallible information? Perhaps paradoxically, this need stems from a kind of skepticism, a lack of confidence in the ability of the human mind to discover necessary truth by reason alone. This is a very different stance from that of the old Deists who believed in a divine Creator but who did not believe in the inspiration of the Bible. Not only did the Bible appear to them a poor candidate for an inspired book, but they believed the Creator had written the only revelation book human beings needed in the world itself, nature, not scripture. And he had given us reason as the only spectacles needful to read and understand it. The biblicist, however, is flustered by over-choice, the condition of being faced with too many options, each with plausible arguments and spokespersons. How is he to decide between them? Suddenly, a religious claim that God has tossed confused humanity the Bible as a life-preserver sounds pretty good. The problem, of course, is that there are just as many competing revelation claims vying for our faith, and one is left without a clue as to deciding between them![108]

But whence the urgency of arriving at true and sure beliefs about all ethical and theological questions? Why not emulate the ancient Skeptics? Like fundamentalist fideists today, the Skeptics viewed the conflict of dogmas from the sidelines and despaired of joining any particular team with confidence. But their conclusion was that such answers, such knowledge, must not be either available or necessary, that one can live perfectly well in this life on the basis of common sense and mere probabilities. Why does our biblicist not adopt the same attitude? I think it is because he holds an unexamined assumption, perhaps a vestige of childhood catechism, a picture of God as some sort of punitive theology professor who stands ready to flunk you if you write the wrong answers on your theology exam. You die and appear at the Pearly Gates, and God hands you the blue book. You do your best on the Theology and Metaphysics final, but if you make enough mistakes, the floor is going to open beneath your feet, as it did beneath old Korah's, and you are going to slide down the shaft to hell. This is a God who does not excuse honest mistakes. Again, I can understand this obnoxious God-concept only as a matter of psychology, not as the implication of any orthodox theology. What element of theology implies that God should be unfair, even peevish? To think him so is to project a childish fear of retribution which can only stifle intellectual growth. Surely it is a legacy of retrograde education, whether religious or secular.

---

108. Walter Kaufmann, *The Faith of a Heretic* (Garden City: Doubleday Anchor Books, 1963), p. 86.

A prime example of this fearful skepticism that needs God's word to settle issues too important for mere human minds to decide would be abortion. It is a difficult matter precisely because of the ambiguities of the issue. Strong cases may be made on various sides of the issue. That fact alone inclines many toward a pro-choice position. But some fundamentalists feel the stakes are high enough that those on the wrong side of the issue, especially abortion doctors, may be justifiably murdered. How can they be so sure they are right? Because God has told them so in the Bible. And this despite the fact that the question of abortion never even comes up in the Bible. The need for the Bible to adjudicate the subject produces the optical illusion that it does.

The need for a sure word from God may simply stem from the kind of intellectual laziness posited by Ludwig Feuerbach. We feel we need to know certain things but are too lazy or impatient to try to figure them out, and the belief in a divine revelation is all too convenient. Convenient both for the lazy one who wants to be spoon-fed, and for the authorities who view themselves as far more capable of finding truth than the laity. But in any case, whether it is a matter of fear or of laziness, I think we may chalk up the desire for "a sure word from God" to a low tolerance for ambiguity.

This is clearly seen in the advice given to pastors and students for studying the Bible. Suppose one is reading the text, seeking divine guidance for one's own life or scriptural grounding for one's beliefs (predestination or free will? Pre- or Post-Tribulation Rapture?). One will shortly discover ambiguity, individual passages that seem to point in one direction or another, or where things are just not so clear. One must then make one's best exegetical judgment call, and then go forward confident that one has achieved the truth. The biblicist awards himself a license for dogmatism, heedless of the necessary tentativeness of one's results. One intends to be dogmatic about whatever conclusions one will wind up embracing. It is just a question of which dogma one will promote. The eager biblicist does not seem to realize that he has simply traded one "uncertain sound" (1 Cor. 14:8) for another: his best guess on the original question for his best guess on the meaning of some biblical verse. There is certainly no reason for him to consider his judgment on the one matter superior to his opinion on the other.

A fear of ambiguity is the chief reason any definitive biblical canon was ever stipulated in the first place: to limit the options for textual divination. God's word and will must be sought only within certain limits. Similarly, this is why the Roman Catholic authorities sought to limit access to the Bible to properly catechized priests who could be trusted to read the text through the spectacles of church tradition. Protestants believed all Christians should be welcome to read the Bible, over-optimistic that the central gospel truth would be clear to all readers. It wasn't, and immediately Protestants had to frame their own creeds to regulate how the Bible might be read and understood—in a good Protestant fashion. The trend continues today as various evangelical seminaries and denominations draft statements of how the Bible may and may not be legitimately interpreted. The goal is to get everyone to agree with the traditional interpretation of the sponsoring group. "Heresy," after all, simply means "choice," the idea being that it is effrontery to choose one's own beliefs rather than submit meekly to spoon-feeding.

What a Tangled Web We Weave
When First We Practice to Believe

I mentioned above that there are liberal theologies of biblical authority that do not entail biblicism. Such theologies often accommodate the possibility that the Bible writers may have contradicted each other. A more liberal theologian might observe that Paul and James disagree over whether faith is sufficient to save one's soul, or whether faith must be realized through works. Such a theologian would consider neither Paul nor James mouthpieces of revelation, both as possible sources of religious wisdom. The theologian's task would be not to submit to either Paul's or James' teaching, but to draw upon both in the process of forming his own (tentative) beliefs. The fundamentalist theologian, by contrast, dismisses the liberal's form of faith as mere speculation, worthless in the face of the ultimate question of salvation. With one's eternal destiny at stake, one must *know*. And thus one needs revelation, not mere speculations whether ancient (James' and Paul's, if that's all they are) or modern (one's own). Since he wants revelation, that is what he is determined to find in the ancient text.

The fundamentalist cannot even recognize that Paul and James contradict one another, since if he did, this would disqualify either or both as mouthpieces of revelation. One might be accepted as a true prophet, the other rejected as a counterfeit, but then who is to decide, and how? Martin Luther had no hesitation in relegating James to the status of a mere appendix to scripture, but most are not so bold. A statement is authoritative for the fundamentalist simply because it appears somewhere in the canon of scripture, all canonical texts being equally authoritative. This is what the slogan "plenary inspiration" means. Unlike in liberal theology, no parts of the Bible are deemed superior or inferior to others. The biblicist, remember, wants to be able just to open the Bible and find his answer. If it is up to him and his meager human abilities to weigh and choose, he is back to square one. He does not want to have to make decisions like this! That's the whole point!

But he cannot escape the horns of dilemmas like this. Fundamentalists follow Martin Luther in wanting to interpret the text of scripture literally, or according to the "plain sense," what it apparently means by straightforward exegesis, such as one would apply to any ancient text. The Bible is inspired, but this only means that its message, once determined by exegesis, must be heeded. Inspiration does not entitle us to read the Bible in some esoteric way, as medieval Catholics did, discerning all manner of secret meanings between the lines. If the Bible may be taken to mean just about anything, then the Bible becomes a Rorschach blot. Again, as a literalist, the biblicist wants to banish ambiguity. Reading the text in a careful and "literal" way, however, sooner or later discloses "apparent contradictions" like those between Paul and James. And at this point the biblicist abandons literalism, falling back to a less-than-literal reading. Suddenly one may and must read between the lines after all. An exception to the straightforward reading is allowed when otherwise the two texts would negate each other's authority and inspiration, a collapse that would take the whole canon with it.

But the cure is worse than the disease! Whatever a "real contradiction" might be, "apparent contradictions" are quite sufficient to vitiate a doctrine of biblical authority that is based on the supposedly "apparent" reading of the text. And it is not just a technicality. For the poor biblicist finds himself situated like the proverbial donkey between the two haystacks: he must decide whether it is Paul or James who is to be taken literally, and which is to be read in a looser way as if he agreed with the other. Though the phrase used is that one must "interpret the less clear texts by the more clear texts," the biblicist is really interpreting the text he *doesn't* like as if it said the same thing as the one he *does* like. In short, he is in precisely the same position as the liberal theologian, choosing between biblical voices; he just doesn't realize it.

How can he continue in such self-deception? Simply because his choice is an automatic one, determined in advance by his particular church's tradition of interpretation. If he were a Catholic, he would read Paul as agreeing with James. As a Protestant, he reads James as echoing Paul once you "really understand" him. The biblicist is submitting to authority, all right, but it is not as he imagines the authority of the text but rather that of his church. And this, too, is fatal, since the first principle of the biblicist is *Sola Scriptura*: "Scripture alone!"

It is such gross, vitiating contradictions that reveal the origin of biblicism to be essentially nontheological. If it had been theological in origin, it would have more consistency. To call on a related field of supernaturalist belief, we might compare biblicism to astrology. A survey of horoscope readers in Britain revealed that most of them admitted the newspaper predictions proved accurate less than half the time. Why then did they continue to read the horoscope? If it were a matter of theoretical consistency, the utter failure of astrology would have been quickly evident. But it was not a matter of theory. It was a matter of psychology: the astrology believers really sought, not knowledge of the future, but rather peace of mind for the night, permission to sleep well in the confidence of being forewarned and thus forearmed for the morrow. When the morrow came and the prediction, probably forgotten, turned out not to prepare them for events, it hardly mattered. They were competent to deal with the day's surprises, but the night before they felt they needed an edge, and reading their horoscope allowed them to imagine they had it. Even so with the biblicist. What he wants from the Bible is not so much a coherent system for divining infallible revelations, but only the permission to dogmatize, whether the goal is to quiet his own fears or to push others around.

A Mighty Fortress Is Our Mentality

Once one has adopted the belief that the Bible must function as the final authority in all matters, some strange results follow. Above, I gave abortion as an example of how the desire for a sure word of revelation leads some biblicists to imagine that the Bible speaks to issues of which it is in fact innocent. To do this is what I call *hermeneutical ventriloquism*. The biblicist may chant "The Bible said it! I believe it! That settles it!" But in practice this often amounts to "I said it! The Bible believes it! That settles it!" One does the scripture the dubious favor of attributing to it one's own beliefs. The (psycho)logical process goes like this: "My opinion is true. The Bible teaches the truth. Therefore the Bible must teach my opinion." One suspects that the dogmatist has simply become so accustomed to dogmatizing that appealing to the Bible is just his way of asserting the truth of his opinion, wherever he got it. Saying "The Bible says" is tantamount to saying, "Verily I say unto thee . . ."

One's imaginary possession of the word of God, or the mind of God, allows the biblicist to wield what I call the Prophetic Ramrod, an attitude of invulnerable narrow-mindedness: "Friend, there is *your* view, and then there is *God's* view."

Such dogmatism may even rub off onto areas where the biblicist feels no especial need to quote the Bible or knows he cannot, areas such as party politics or even selling merchandise. Whether one is "witnessing" to the glories of Christian salvation, Amway products or Mary Kay Cosmetics, one uses the same methods (as Southern Baptist salesman and evangelist Zig Ziglar freely admits in his book *Secrets of Closing the Sale*).

The Sliding Scale of Biblical Inerrancy

Another anomaly resulting from the psychological, not theological, basis of biblicism is the shifting opinion of biblicists over the years as to what the allegedly infallible teaching of the Bible actually *is* when it comes to the world of nature. There was a time when readers of the Bible could see quite well that it "taught" (or presupposed) a flat earth that floated on water, covered by a solid firmament (dome) that kept out another ocean above. The earth was orbited by the sun and supported by pillars. And every Bible reader understood this. In the name of the infallible Bible, religious authorities opposed the progress of science. Today, most fundamentalists reject evolution because it contradicts the Bible. But only a tiny minority still believe the earth is flat. A slightly larger minority believe that the sun orbits the earth. Most fundamentalists believe that the earth is round and that it orbits the sun. And they do not even realize that the biblical picture of the earth contradicts these notions. Their religious upbringing has told them that the Bible contradicts science only at the point of evolution. As for the rest, they have even been told that the ancient writers of the Bible miraculously foreknew what it took modern science centuries to learn, that the earth is round, that it orbits the sun, etc. These assertions are read into the Bible by forced and implausible readings of various passages out of context, akin to attempts to show that the Bible writers knew about flying saucers. The true teaching of the Bible on these matters, they say, could not be understood until modern science allowed us to understand the relevant texts correctly! This is very close to (but also very far from) a frank admission of the game of catch-up being played here.

But what makes the difference between whether one recognizes contradictions between the Bible and science or one pretends the Bible anticipated modern science? It is simply peer pressure, massive and permeating public opinion. Ancient biblicists lived in a peer group (a "plausibility structure," as Peter Berger would call it) that believed in a flat earth orbited by the sun, created in a week. It would have been hard to believe anything radically different. As the plausibility structure shifted, so that most people in the culture no longer took the ancient world-picture seriously, it ceased to be an option for biblicists to retain the biblical cosmology. They couldn't withstand the cognitive peer pressure. And today the great majority, including biblicists, believe in a round, sun-orbiting earth, but it is not so obvious to the great majority that all life forms gradually evolved from a common ancestor. One still has breathing room on that point; one can still afford to recognize what the Bible says. One can still, for the time being, reject evolution and not seem a freak. The fundamentalist dreads the time when universal belief might turn to accept evolution, and so they seek to defer that day by means of public debates, censoring biology textbooks, etc. Their effort is not to persuade the intelligentsia (scientists) of the truth of anti-evolutionism, but rather to appeal to the gallery in the manner of a political campaign. They are looking for "votes" in order to retain an amenable plausibility structure. It is all psychological, not theological, since what the Bible says or does not say about the natural world is utterly beside the point. The day will eventually come when biblicists will reinterpret Genesis to teach evolution and will claim that God had revealed it to the ancient scriptural writers ages before scientists discovered it. And these new scriptural "insights" will have come not from exegesis but solely from social peer pressure.

Hermeneutical Ventriloquism

Allegory is tied into the doctrine of the *plenary inspiration* of a *canonized scripture*. Allegory is often or even fundamentally employed to impart theological/edifying significance to those passages which seem to have none, texts that would be superfluous otherwise.

> Any technique of exposition or exegesis which will establish every word of the Bible on an exalted plane is acceptable to the cabalist. Such exaltation is a necessity, for there is much in the Bible which is too trivial to be the work of the Supreme Intelligence. It is necessary to determine the hidden meanings lying behind superficial trivialities.[109]

---

109. Joseph Leon Blau, *The Christian Interpretation of the Cabala in the Renaissance* (NY: Columbia University Press,

> Are we to imagine that Almighty God who was giving answers to Moses from heaven made regulations about an oven, a frying-pan and a baking-pan? (Origen, *Homily on Leviticus* 5:5)[110]

But if we reject such a doctrine of scripture, not only do we not have the right to look for such esoteric meanings, but we also lack the need to. If some piece of text is dead wood, so be it. Who cares! We must approach the task with a new and scientific understanding.

Allegory also serves to press old scripture into service in behalf of a new theology not taught in it. It is a way of *rewriting* the old by *rereading* it. The motive is to provide (spurious) credentials for the new doctrines by seeming to find them after all in the old scripture. The three men who showed up at Abraham's campfire were the Trinity, etc.

Is allegory telling us anything? It seems not. It is not as if there is a method whereby new information may be mined from the text. It is always a matter of clever illustration as rhetorical reinforcement of something we already knew. While one might conceivably use *gematria*, etc., to "find" unprecedented things from the text, it does not work that way. Instead, whether explicitly or implicitly, the rule of (whichever) faith is always invoked as a limit to the kind of thing that may be found by allegorical means. And this means one will only be seeking spurious scriptural credentials (proof texts) for doctrines one already believes on other grounds.

1944), p. 5.

110. Quoted in R.P.C. Hanson, *Allegory and Event: A Study of the Sources and Significance of Origen's Interpretation of Scripture* (Richmond: Westminster/John Knox Press, rpt. 2002), pp. 219–220.

I venture to say that even in cases of some "heretic" using allegory or *gematria* to produce genuinely new doctrines (*ipso facto* heresies), we would find he is reading in some notion he has already formulated philosophically or received in a vision, etc. The way it works, you have to be looking for something already. I believe any impartial reader of, say, Charles Fillmore's *Metaphysical Bible Dictionary*[111] will agree that it is a collection of clever attempts to reduce every text to a reiteration of New Thought doctrine that itself was not first derived from any sort of esoteric reading, but rather from straightforward, literal readings of certain key texts (especially Mark 11:22–24 and Acts 17:28) which then form the basis for the interpretation (actually, *re*interpretation) of all other texts. This is always the logic and process of allegory.

What allegory does (and, again the *Metaphysical Bible Dictionary* is a prime example) is to pick up on certain fortuitous parallels in word, action, or logical pattern between a text (or even an etymology) and a doctrine, story, or (theo) logical sequence. Then it says the literal scriptural instance is a shell or cocoon for the more abstract notion for which rootage in scripture is being sought. It results only in pleasant, sometimes striking--but coincidental—scriptural allusions. That's all. Sermon illustrations.

When we look at Genesis, we might read Platonism into the creation story as Philo did, but to what purpose? He was trying to make Platonism legitimate in the eyes of fellow Jews. He pretended that Plato had derived his system from Moses! No more than a propaganda stunt that twists the text, albeit

111. Charles Fillmore, *Metaphysical Bible Dictionary*. Charles Fillmore Reference Library (Lee's Summit, MO: Unity School of Christianity, 1995).

in admittedly very clever ways. Or we might find in Genesis One a symbolic tracing of the stages of development of human consciousness, as per both Swedenborg and the *Metaphysical Bible Dictionary*. But do we really learn it there? Or have we not already formulated it philosophically or psychologically? Are we not just reading it into the text?

The many cases where Matthew and other New Testament writers tell us that so and so Old Testament prophecy was fulfilled in Jesus represent ancient *pesher* ("puzzle solution") exegesis, akin to allegory. The operative assumption is that the Holy Spirit caused the ancient writers to prophesy on two levels. One was germane to their day and understandable in literal terms by their contemporaries. The other was a hidden prediction of Jesus which could not be recognized as such until after the fact, and from the standpoint of Christian faith. But, again, this seems entirely tautological: it contributes nothing new. We discover nothing from the prophetic text we did not already know from Christian preaching about Jesus.

It should come as no surprise that theologians and interpreters in all religions have had occasion sooner or later to resort to allegorical interpretation in view of two facts common to all faiths. First, their scriptures, having been written over many centuries by various hands, do not agree theologically with one another. Second, religious thought continues to evolve, and authorization must be sought in the old scriptures for the new opinions; therefore theologians find new ways of reading the old texts that will cause them to (seem to) yield new truths.

I Buried Paul

Gershom Scholem makes remarks that apply to our subject matter regardless of which religion we are talking about.

Paul had a mystical experience which he interpreted in such a way that it shattered the traditional authority. He could not keep it intact; but since he did not wish to forego the authority of the Holy Scriptures as such, he was forced to declare that it was limited in time and hence abrogated. A purely mystical exegesis of the old words replaced the original frame and provided the foundation of the new authority which he felt called upon to establish. This mystic's clash with religious authority was clear and sharp. In a manner of speaking, Paul read the Old Testament 'against the grain.' The incredible violence with which he did so shows not only how incompatible his experience was with the meaning of the old books, but also how determined he was to preserve, if only by purely mystical exegeses, his bond with the sacred text. The result was the paradox that never ceases to amaze us when we read the Pauline Epistles: on the one hand the Old Testament is preserved, on the other, its meaning is completely set aside. The new authority that is set up, for which the Pauline Epistles themselves serve as a holy text, is revolutionary in nature. Having found a new source, it breaks away from the authority constituted in Judaism, but continues in part to clothe itself in the images of the old authority, which has been reinterpreted in purely spiritual terms.[112]

---

112. Gershom Scholem, "Religious Authority and Mysticism," in Scholem, *On the Kabbalah and its Symbolism*. Trans. Ralph Manheim (NY: Schocken Books, 1969), pp. 14–15.

It is generally known that allegorical interpretations arise spontaneously whenever a conflict between new ideas and those expressed in a sacred book necessitates some form of compromise. What is true of allegorical interpretation is still more applicable to the specifically mystical interpretation of such texts.[113]

Actually the thought processes of mystics are largely unconscious, and they may be quite unaware of the clash between old and new which is of such passionate interest to the historian. They are thoroughly steeped in the religious tradition in which they have grown up, and many notions which strike a modern reader as fantastic distortions of a text spring from a conception of Scripture which to the mystic seems perfectly natural.[114]

Similarity of purpose and hence in the fundamental structure of the mystical ideas about the Holy Scriptures accounts for the parallels between certain Kabbalistic statements about the Torah and those of Islamic mystics about the Koran or of Christian mystics about their Biblical canon.[115]

"Kabbalah" simply means "tradition" but denotes a particular strand of Jewish mystical tradition, called "the Lore of Creation." It dates back to about the second to third century CE, as far as we can tell. Its chief documents include the *Sepher*

---

113. Scholem, "The Meaning of the Torah in Jewish Mysticism," in *On the Kabbalah and its Symbolism*, p. 33.

114. Scholem, "The Meaning of the Torah in Jewish Mysticism," p. 33.

115. Scholem, "The Meaning of the Torah in Jewish Mysticism," p. 35.

Yetsirah (Book of Creation, second–third century), the *Bahir* (late twelfth century), and the encyclopedic compendium of mystical Torah commentary, the *Zohar* (Book of Splendor). This last is the work of a Spanish Rabbi, Moses de Leon, at the start of the thirteenth century CE.

Before the *Zohar* dominated the scene, there were three major Kabbalistic movements. First, Isaac the Blind, active 1190–1210, with his disciples Ezra and Azarael, lived in Southern France and Spain. They developed the doctrine of the world emanating from God (see below). They also suggested the doctrine of metempsychosis/reincarnation. Second, Eliezar of Worms (active ca. 1220) and his disciples introduced numerical and alphabetical techniques (though they had existed way back into the second century CE at least). Third, Abraham ben Samuel Abulafia (1240-ca. 1292), a self-proclaimed messiah, combined and further refined the elements of his predecessors, both theoretically and practically (i.e., devotionalism and scriptural study). His disciple Joseph ben Abraham Gikatilia (ca. 1247–1305) was the greatest systematizer yet and greatly developed the three famous techniques of esoteric interpretation widely used by their followers, including later Hasidic Jews, for the purpose of finding their beloved Kabbalistic doctrines in scripture. They are:

> "*Gematria*, i.e., the calculation of the numerical value of Hebrew words and the search for connections with other words or phrases of equal values."[116] "It involved the use of the fact that in ancient languages, including

---

116.Gershom Scholem, "Hasidism in Medieval Germany." Trans. George Lichtheim. Third Lecture, *Major Trends in Jewish Mysticism* (NY: Schocken Books, 193), p. 100).

Hebrew, the letters of the alphabet also represented numbers. This suggested that, when the sum of the numerical equivalents of the letters of two or more words was the same, the words might be considered identical and used interchangeably."[117]

"*Notarikon* [was the] interpretation of the letters of a word as abbreviations of whole sentences."[118]

The initial or final letters of the words of a phrase might be joined to form a word which was then given occult significance. The significance of another word might be explained by expanding it into a phrase, using each letter of the original as [the] initial letter of one word of the phrase. Finally, two words might be joined as one and thus given new meaning.[119]

"*Temurah* [was the] interchange of letters according to certain systematic rules"[120]

Themurah, which means "transposition," is actually a combination of the letter substitutions of the code and the anagrammatic interchange of the resultant letters. Since an alphabet of twenty-two consonants provides twenty-one codes, and since vowel sounds

---

117. Blau, *Christian Interpretation*, p. 8.

118. Scholem, "Hasidism in Medieval Germany," p. 100.

119. Blau, *Christian Interpretation*, p. 8.

120. Scholem, "The Meaning of the Torah in Jewish Mysticism," p. 35.

are not printed in Hebrew, an almost infinite number of letter combinations can be produced from any one Hebrew word, and some few of these combinations are likely to form words. This method, then, is likely to be fruitful.[121]

Moses de Leon, author of the *Zohar* and the *Pardes* (Paradise), counted four separate levels of meaning in the Torah and listed them in a pun on "Pardes."

P for *peshat*, "designating the literal or simple meaning, which is preserved even in the mystical transfiguration, though it has been made transparent by the mystical light shining through it."[122]

R stands for *remez*, the allegorical meaning.

D stands for *derasha* (cf. *Midrash*), the haggadic or Talmudic meaning (legal, casuistic interpretation).

S stands for *sod*, the mystical meaning referring to the secrets of the Divine Attributes, the Heavenly Adam, the Creation, etc.

Later he added *Gematria* as a fifth, though it was more a means of unlocking the others, not a separate level of meaning in its own right.

---

121. Blau, *Christian Interpretation*, pp. 8–9; Scholem, "The Meaning of the Torah in Jewish Mysticism," p. 35.

122. Scholem, "The Meaning of the Torah in Jewish Mysticism," p. 56.

I hasten to note that the complex cosmology and spirituality produced by such techniques must be evaluated according to whatever worth Jewish mystics find in them, just as in the case of the Christian gospels despite the divination methods employed by the evangelists. But as for these divinatory gimmicks themselves, I think we must mark them as religious superstition. This comes into very clear focus in the discussions of evangelical biblical scholars like Gordon Fee and Richard Longenecker. They do not flinch at admitting the difficulty of the situation. They hold the belief that the whole Bible is inspired by God, but they are good Protestants who would not dream of treating the Old Testament the way the New Testament writers (or the later Jewish Kabbalists) did. Like Martin Luther, Fee and Longenecker insist on grammatico-historical exegesis, a straightforward reading of authorial intention in what they wrote insofar as we can figure that out. This is the only way to safeguard against the use of the Bible as a ventriloquist dummy. But in this they are eschewing the methods of the New Testament writers themselves: esoteric, non-literal exegesis! So how do they rationalize this seeming contradiction? By what psychologists call "eccentricity credits." They say that Eleanor Roosevelt once showed up to a luncheon wearing blue jeans (or some such indecorous garb). Though any other guest doing this would be shown the door at once (Matt. 22:11–13), the First Lady can get away with it: "She, ah, feels more comfortable this way." So would everybody else, but unfortunately they're not married to the President. In the same way, Fee and Longenecker[123] figure, with implicit chagrin, that

---

123. Richard Longenecker, *Biblical Exegesis in the Apostolic Period*. (Grand Rapids: Eerdmans, 1975), pp. 218–220; Gordon Fee, class lectures at Gordon-Conwell Theological Seminary, May, 1978.

if you're a New Testament writer, you can get away with it. That is, believers in biblical inspiration have to accept that somehow Matthew was right in seeing a secret prediction in Hosea 11:1 of the Holy Family's sojourn in Egypt.[124] This, even though we can laugh at Justin Martyr taking Isaiah 50:6, "I gave my cheeks to those who pluck the beard," as prophetically confirming that Jesus wore facial hair. You can just hear evangelical scholars heaving a sigh of relief that *this* wasn't in the New Testament canon! But it's too late. Are they not obligated to recognize in the apostolic text-twisting a legitimization of ancient non-literal exegesis in principle? Otherwise, it's "Bultmann, here we come!" The fact that even (some) evangelical scholars feel compelled to bracket off the type of biblical interpretation used by the writers themselves doubly attests the superstitious character of this aspect of biblical authority: on the one hand, they can't accept it; on the other, they dare not explicitly repudiate it.

Fee is quite consistent, however, when he attacks the use of scripture by Prosperity Gospel gurus like Kenneth Copeland as "almost totally subjective, and comes not from study but from 'meditation,' which in Copeland's case means a kind of free association based on a prior commitment to his—totally wrong—understanding of the 'basic' texts."[125] Charismatic preachers distinguish between God's "word" as *logos*, referring to the letter of the sacred text, and as *rhema*, the "living and active" communication from God to the individual reader, an illumination that goes beyond the literal meaning, using the

124. Krister Stendahl, *The School of St. Matthew and Its Use of the Old Testament* (Philadelphia: Fortress Press, 1968).

125. Gordon D. Fee, *The Disease of the Health & Wealth Gospels* (Costa Mesa: The Word for Today, 1979), pp.5–6.

text as a springboard for "fresh light to break forth" (if you'll forgive the mixed metaphor). Of course, this is the source of the Big Bucks gospel teaching. And it amounts to sheer superstition, an oracular manipulation of the Bible.

Nor is that the only oracular use of scripture popular among Christians today. There is a long and embarrassing history of evangelical and fundamentalist attempts to match out-of-historical-context verses from Daniel, Ezekiel, Revelation, and the Olivet Discourse (Mark 13 and parallels) with modern political and military developments in the Middle East.[126] Hal Lindsey might as well be the reincarnation of one of the Dead Sea Scrolls sectarians who decoded, e.g., Habakkuk, as a set of predictions of the advent of their guru, the Teacher of Righteousness. Lindsey[127] saw in the scriptures prophecies of the Common Market, the USSR, the Peoples' Republic of China, etc. Multitudes read Lindsey's screed and breathlessly awaited the Rapture, after which, from the heavenly bleachers, they should enjoy the spectacle of the Great Tribulation, presumably munching on manna popcorn. Some of his readers were so sure there would be no mundane future that they cancelled plans for enrolling in college. We saw the same sort of fanaticism, based on outrageous exegetical sleight of hand, in the recent embarrassments of Harold Camping and his gullible legions. How strange to see ostensible literalists staking everything on wildly extravagant interpretations far beyond any straightforward exegesis!

---

126. Dwight Wilson, *Armageddon Now! The Premillenarian Response to Russia and Israel since 1917* (Grand Rapids: Baker Book House, 1977).

127. Hal Lindsey with C.C. Carlson, *The Late Great Planet Earth* (NY: Bantam Books, 1973).

A related trend is the fascination with "the Bible Code," a computerized Kabbalism that thinks to find coded predictions in the Bible by searching the vast text for letters occurring at arbitrarily selected intervals. If, once collected, these letters chance to form words and phrases in the original languages, these may form Nostradamus-like hints of things to come. All this is of a piece with the 1970s hysteria over "backward masking," the belief that rock musicians had somehow encoded secret messages backwards and that playing the record in reverse would reveal these messages from Satan. I suppose one could imagine mischievous rockers pulling such a stunt ("Be sure to drink your Ovaltine") just to pique interest among adolescent fans. But can we really imagine Almighty God bothering with such stuff? Is not such a deity obviously the projection of the mentality of geeks and nerds like the bunch of pencil-necked hermaphrodites on *The Big Bang Theory*? Goodbye, God of the Gaps; hello, God of the Geeks.

Worse still is the letter-counting of Ivan Panin,[128] still often read and sworn by today. Panin maintained that the Hebrew and Greek texts of the Bible were composed of ubiquitous number patterns beneath the surface narratives and teachings, patterns with no inherent meaning but proving the divine inspiration of the Bible since its writers could not have been aware of it themselves. They weren't trying to compose on the basis of number patterns; it just worked out that way thanks to divine providence. So you better take what the Bible says seriously, mister! Someone is missing the forest for the trees here! And if this strange business is what it takes to convince you of the

---

128. Herbert Dennett, *A Guide to Modern Versions of the New Testament: How to Understand and Use Them* (Chicago: Moody Press, 1966), pp. 79–80.

authority of scripture, this and not the evident profundity of so much of it, well, there's word for you: "superstitious."

Ignorance, Injustice, and Adversity

Superstition "may . . . serve the positive function of giving the person at least the feeling of having some control; although illusory, this may well help to preserve the integrity of the personality."[129] This insight, I think, applies equally to religion insofar as religion partakes of superstition, and the more it does, the more superstitious it is. Anthropologist Clifford Geertz[130] explains the psychological utility of religion, pretty much *any* religion, in maintaining a sense of composure in the face of life's uncertainties. Religions, he says, are cultural symbol-systems which help us deal with three major perennial challenges: ignorance, adversity, and injustice. This it does by reassuring us that everything makes sense (or will make sense) in an unseen realm of space or time adjacent to this one.

We are left without any evident answers to certain deep questions, such as the fate of the individual after death. But Spiritualist mediums can tell us, and we want to believe them. Bible believers are worried about contradictions in scripture. When strained rationalizations fail, believers take comfort in the assurance that, after death, there will be a big seminar in which professorial angels will iron them out in clever ways we

129. Gustav Jahoda, *The Psychology of Superstition*. Pelican Books (Baltimore: Penguin Books, 1970), p. 146.

130. Clifford Geertz, "Religion as a Cultural System" in William A. Lessa and Evon Z. Vogt, eds., *Reader in Comparative Religion: An Anthropological Approach* (NY: Harper & Row, 1972), pp. 167–178.

never thought of. Okay, we still don't have a solution, but at least we "know" there will be one someday.

Why do the wicked so often escape punishment? Why no justice for the oppressed and the victims of crime? Religion tells us not to worry, for the wicked will wake up in hell fire, while the oppressed righteous will receive ample reward in heaven. Or the wicked will be reincarnated as maggots, while the righteous will dwell in celestial palaces, or at least receive a bump up to a better caste. So things will be evened up in the invisible world above us or before us.

What to make of injury and adversity? What if your name is Job? How can this stuff be happening to him? Well, he never finds out, but we know he was the object of a little experiment conducted up in the sky by Jehovah and Satan. Have you ever been to a funeral reception and heard people piously reassure one another, "He's here; he's here, all right." In an invisible zone, of course. What, Jesus didn't return on schedule? Uh, *sure* he did, only invisibly, just beyond the blue sky. Religion, then, constructs a vast, invisible empire of pure supposition for which there is no evidence.[131] As the product of wishful, magical thinking, I call it superstition.

---

131. See the catalog of theodicy rationalizations discussed in Peter L. Berger, *The Sacred Canopy: Elements of a Sociological Theory of Religion* (Garden City: Doubleday Anchor Books, 1969), Chapter 3, "The Problem of Theodicy," pp. 53–80.

Chapter Eight

The Retreat from Radical Prayer

Rabbi Zwi Chaim Yisroel [was] an Orthodox scholar of the Torah and a man who developed whining to an art unheard of in the West. Once ... he was on his way to synagogue to celebrate the sacred Jewish holiday commemorating God reneging on every promise ...[132]

Frazer, as we have seen, believed that magic gave way to religion when the supposedly sure-fire operations of the magician proved unreliable and unpredictable. Tapping into unseen forces obeying supernatural laws, the incantations, rain dances, etc., *had* to work. But too often they *didn't*. So they went back to the drawing board. Religion posited a different paradigm for interpreting experience: instead of ineluctable and invariable laws, religion envisioned personal wills of

---

132. Woody Allen, "Hassidic Tales" in Allen, *Getting Even* (NY: Vintage Books, 1978), p. 50.

invisible superhuman entities. One could not command them. One might only petition them, hoping for one's request to be granted but fully aware that it might not be. The improvement was not in better results. It was still hit-and-miss, but this no longer debunked the system. That's why it was deemed better. We regard magic as superstition, religion as at least compatible with a more sophisticated worldview. But religion can easily backslide into magic and superstition. The Bible warns of this danger when it tells us not to "tempt the Lord your God," to presume upon him. But the Bible itself sometimes backslides into superstition, telling us we can make some tall demands on God, appealing to God's faithfulness to his promises as our excuse. And then the biblical writers have to start back-pedaling. It is a fascinating process to trace.

The New Testament Evolution

The primary text dealing with answered prayer is of course Mark 11:22–24: "And answering, Jesus says to them, 'Have faith in God. Amen: I tell you that whoever says to this mountain, "Up and into the sea with you!" and believes that what he says happens, it will be granted to him. In view of that, I tell you, all things for which you pray and ask, believe that they are yours, and your request will be granted you.'"). Upon this rock, I maintain, is built the whole edifice of "name it and claim it" prayer, "blank check" prayer. The proposition is as simple as it is radical: I ask, God grants, and I can be sure he will.

Is it a magic formula? No, for there is already an escape clause: one must believe the request will be granted. It is almost a Zen statement;[133] one must have set aside all considerations of worldly probability and expectation, as Romans 4:17–21 says Abraham did, or no heir would have been forthcoming. The logic is this: nothing shall be considered impossible for God. Once God enters the equation, all bets are off. Or rather, they are *on*. It is no longer either impossible or unlikely that your prayer will be realized, since it is nothing for God to do it. He will not even work up a sweat. Why *not* believe he will do it?

From this summit of believing expectation we witness a gradual decline through the pages of the New Testament, like the returning dullness of the disciples, as their stupid questions show, as they descend the Mount of Transfiguration with the no-longer glowing Jesus. We detect clear signs of a shrinking confidence in prayer. Why this decline? It is no mystery. This retreat from radical prayer is only the cooling of sectarian zeal typical for all new religious movements. As time goes by, once-sizzling believers sink back into complacent conformity with the norms of the society and religion against which they first stood out like a sore thumb. One cannot maintain fever-pitch zeal forever as long as one must live in a world that is not evidently coming to a crashing end in the near future. There are bills to pay, family to be provided for, civic obligations to mind. Religion retreats to a sideline, a hobby, a pursuit to which one regrets one cannot devote more energy. If a select few want to maintain their "first love" in all its fervor, there will be special arrangements for them: monasteries, convents, etc. These are special environments mimicking the Kingdom of God these

133. Joseph Chilton Pearce, *The Crack in the Cosmic Egg: Challenging Constructs of Mind and Reality* (NY: Pocket Books, 1973), pp. 176–177.

few wish they lived in, with no worldly distractions, like the Holodeck on *Star Trek.*

Everyone else retreats to a stance that Reinhold Niebuhr called "Christian Realism."[134] It proves impractical to heed literally those radical gospel mandates including non-retaliation in wartime, abandoning worldly security, donating all worldly goods to the poor (thereby joining their number, along with one's family who probably weren't in on the decision!). With the compromises one forfeits the old confidence in promises (real or imagined) of prayer for healing, for sinless sanctification, for Spirit-inspired boldness in witnessing. All these come to be thought of as "relevant but impossible ideals."[135] They play the role of the North Star: guiding the way, but not in itself a credible destination. One is too much in the world to live every day in the fantasy world of a Jesus movie.

Perhaps the closest New Testament parallel to the retreat from radical prayer would be the early expectation of the Parousia, the second coming of Christ. We start with gospel promises that the end will dawn before the generation of Jesus' contemporaries has expired: Mark 13:30, "This generation will not pass away till all these things are fulfilled." But time went by and nothing happened. Many died. So now we read a hedged version of the promise: "*Some* standing here will not taste death till they see the kingdom of God having come with power" (Mark 9:1). Eventually the available witness pool shrank to one single survivor: "It was rumored among the brethren that this disciple was not to die" (John 21:23a). But then *he* died, and it

---

134. Reinhold Niebuhr, *An Interpretation of Christian Ethics.* Living Age Books (NY: Meridian Books, 1956), p. 130.

135. Niebuhr, *Interpretation of Christian Ethics*, Chapter 4, "The Relevance of an Impossible Ethical Ideal," pp. 97–123.

was time to reinterpret the promise again! "But Jesus did not actually *say* he was not going to die, only that if he so willed, it was no one else's business" (John 21:23b).

And then the ridicule set in with a vengeance: "First of all, be sure of this: *in the last days, mockers will appear, following their own lusts,* making wisecracks, saying things like, 'What happened to the promise of his coming? After all, from the day the fathers fell asleep, all remains as it was since the dawn of creation!'" (2 Pet. 3:3–4). The answer? "But, brothers, don't you let this fact be concealed from you: 'One day for the Lord is the same as a millennium, and a millennium as a single day.' It is not so much that the Lord is tardy fulfilling his promise, as some define tardiness. No, it is that he is long-suffering toward you, unwilling for any to perish and hoping everyone will come to their senses" (2 Pet. 3:8–9). Sure, it's a delay, wiseass, but you ought to be grateful for it! It's a reprieve! Not bad reasoning, but the tendency is nonetheless clear: a retreat from imminent expectation of the Parousia to the calm belief that, yes, it will happen *some* day. In the meantime, don't take advantage of the delay. Don't give up hope. This is the point of the parables of the Lazy Steward (Matt. 24:45–51) and the Wise and Foolish Virgins (Matt. 25:1–13).

Another parallel: think of Mark 9:28–29, "And when [after an exorcism,] he entered into a house, his disciples questioned him privately: 'Why were we unable to cast it out?' And he told them. 'This particular species can come out by means of nothing but prayer. [And, if that doesn't work, fasting].'" The story came to be used in the early church as a formula for exorcism,[136] but

---

136. Davies, *Revolt of the Widows*, pp. 22–23, referring to Origen, *Contra Celsum* 1.46. See also Raphael Patai, *The Hebrew Goddess* (NY: Avon/Discus Books, 1978), pp. 188–189, for the similar use of Elijah stories in medieval Jewish

mere recitation of the story of Jesus' triumph did not do the trick after a while (if it ever had), so someone started fine-tuning, adding *prayer* as a condition for success with deaf-mute epilepsy demons. When this, too, proved ineffective after a while, some scribes began to add the stipulation of *fasting* for the exorcist-in-training before "the big match." It is the same sort of pious back- pedaling we are gauging with prayer.

Even closer, though from another religious tradition, would be the failure of Shankara's promise that simply understanding the major Upanishadic statements of Nondualism must issue in immediate enlightenment. It turned out not to be so simple:

> Samkaracarya declared that the cognitive understanding of the meaning of the four great Upanisadic dicta, "this *atma* is *brahma*", "I am *brahma*", "thou art that", and "the conscious self is *brahma*", results in immediate liberation. Most of his contemporaries and particularly his later opponents ... opposed this notion vehemently, insisting on prolonged observance and discipline.[137]

Why? Obviously because, even though some people managed to understand the concept of the thing, nothing happened. The promised enlightenment, a mystical experience of one's unity with the Godhead, did not occur. Thus many decided some further steps must be necessary to clear away the clouds of worldly ignorance.[138]

---

exorcism rites.

137. Bharati, *Tantric Tradition*, pp. 19–20.

138. See L. Thomas O'Neil, *Maya in Sankara: Measuring the Immeasurable* (Dehli: Motilal Banarsidass, 1980), Chapter Five, "Maya in the Post-Sankara Advaita," pp. 96–124.

I said there is a second reason for the decline from religious radicalism, and that is *a gradual coming to terms with reality*. The experiment of faith just fails, and one learns the lesson ruefully. Henceforth one's expectations are not so great. One whittles down the promises enough that even tepid faith may grasp them, not that there is much of a pay-off to be had. One tells oneself that it was never realistic to expect entire sanctification, miraculous healing, to survive till the second coming, to be provided for even after giving away all one's money, to go out onto the field of battle and be invulnerable to the unbelievers' bullets.[139] Wise up.

Of course, from the believer's standpoint, this is not an awakening to mature realism at all. The true believer will lament that faith has been lost, and with it great treasures to which it might have been the key. I guess the difference between the skeptic and the believer is one's track record: how many times has the believed-for blessing fallen through? But then the question passes over into *theodicy*: can we think of ways to absolve God of the apparent failure of his promises? To make it *our* fault? What we are about to see in our brief survey of other New Testament texts on faith and prayer is a series of *mitigations* of the original promises, the addition of stipulations, provisos, and conditions. The reason they have been added is to vindicate God in the face of the failure of believing prayer. Sure, confidence in prayer is thereby undermined, but even

---

139. Most famous as occurring in the Boxer Rebellion in China, this belief in charismatic invulnerability occurs also in several Asian Indian messianic movements. See Stephen Fuchs, *Rebellious Prophets: A Study of Messianic Movements in Indian Religions*. Publications of the Indian Branch of the Anthropos Institute No. 1 (NY: Asia Publishing House, 1965), pp. 29–30, 32, 41, 96, 98, 107, 123, 149–150, 220.

that is better than blaming God. One Psalmist demands to know: "Why sleepest thou, O Lord?" Another replies, No, "He that guardeth Israel neither slumbers nor sleeps."

Even the repeated delay of the Parousia, like the failure of prayer, has been explained as due to the failure of believers, not of God. This is the point of Acts 3:19–21 ("So repent and turn back, for your sins to be expunged, so times of restoration may arrive from the presence of the Lord and he may send the Christ already appointed for you, Jesus, whom heaven is required to keep until times of restitution of all things, which God spoke about through the mouth of all his holy prophets from antiquity"). If Christ has not returned on schedule it is *our* fault. This is an old notion inherited from Judaism: why does the Messiah not come to relieve Jewish suffering? Because they do not show themselves worthy of his deliverance by keeping the Torah.

Mustard Seed of Doubt

To repeat: a second look at Mark 11:22–24: "Have faith in God. Amen: I tell you that whoever says to this mountain, 'Up and into the sea with you!' and believes that what he says happens, it will be granted to him. In view of that, I tell you, all things for which you pray and ask, believe that they are yours, and your request will be granted you." It suggests that an escape clause has already been inserted to mitigate the easily-disproven boast of the original promise: "And does not doubt in his heart." This condition seems to introduce the element of doubt, injecting a taint into the absolute confidence the saying otherwise means to encourage. One problem is that this condition fatally shifts the focus from what an omnipotent God may do on the one hand, to a mortal's faith on the other. If the believer can muster up enough faith, like Green Lantern summoning up sufficient will power to operate his power ring, he will accomplish the miracle. The believer has replaced God as the wonder-worker. He is answering his own prayer. The pious reader stumbles at the challenge of mountain-moving power and inevitably asks, "Do I have enough faith for *that*? *Could* I?" This is an element of fearful introspection (familiar, I do not doubt, to every one who has ever taken this promise seriously). It saps the pure confidence with which Superman makes his leap from the open window of the *Daily Planet*. When Yoda upbraids Luke Skywalker, telling him that he must not *try* to raise his vehicle from the swamp, that instead he must simply *do* it, he is telling Luke to exorcize that poisonous element of doubt. But Mark 11:23, as I read it, injects the mustard seed, not of *faith*, but of *doubt*, preparing the reader in advance for failure. James 1:6–8 sets up the same booby trap: "Only let him be sure to ask in faith, without ambivalence; for the doubter wavers like the tossing of the sea, driven and tossed by the wind. Such a one need not imagine he is likely to receive anything at all from the Lord, for he is of two minds, habitually indecisive." In the face of this sapping of the positivity of faith, one can only repeat the despairing words of the nameless man in Mark 9:24: "I'm *trying* to believe! Help my *un*belief!"[140] At least, as in C.S. Lewis's *The Screwtape Letters*, that puts an end to the vexing doublethink.[141]

---

140. Here is what I judge the most profound New Testament saying on prayer, and who said it? Jesus? An apostle? A prophet? No, just—*some guy!*

141. Lewis, *Screwtape Letters*, pp. 62–63.

The sort of anxiety I have in mind is exactly paralleled in the agonizing of Pure Land Buddhists who had been taught they need only call upon the name of Amitabha Buddha to guarantee rebirth in the Pure Land, a Buddha-planet created through the good karma of the immortal Bodhisattva where one might attain full enlightenment at once upon arrival there. But any idiot could repeat the words "I call upon Amitabha Buddha." Mustn't there be some special state of mind? Pure Land theoreticians began the long process of debating how much desire for rebirth, how much sorrow for sins, and how much sincerity were required for the meditative recipe to work.[142] Alas, no peace of mind lies *that* way. The same Hall of Mirrors beckons us in John 15:7 ("If you dwell in me and my words dwell in you, ask whatever you wish, and it shall happen for you."): how do you know when and how fully you are dwelling "in Jesus"? Or that his sayings are dwelling, gestating, within your soul? Apparently not deeply enough if your prayers fail. It is a sliding scale that can slide as far as needed to get God off the hook.

Outvoting God

Matthew 18:19–20 says, "Again, I say to you that if two of you agree on earth concerning everything they may ask, it shall happen for them from my Father in the heavens. For where two or three are assembled in my name, I am there in their midst." The verse now forms part of a section of Matthew's

---

142. Alfred Bloom, *Shinran's Gospel of Pure Grace*. Monographs of the Association for Asian Studies (Tucson: University of Arizona Press, 1977), throughout.

gospel devoted to disciplinary matters in the local Christian community. It has much in common with the Dead Sea Scroll called the Community Rule (or Manual of Discipline). As such it must be taken as meaning that disciplinary decisions must be by consensus of a small quorum of two or three, modeled upon the Old Testament requirement of two or three witnesses (Deut. 17:6; 19:15). But it is evident that the saying originally circulated as an independent pericope (a self-contained unit of oral tradition), and it concerned prayer in general. As such it forms another stage of retrenchment in prayer. It introduces another variable upon which failure in prayer may be blamed: did you have enough signatures on the petition to persuade God? This proviso gets God off the hook in one sense (he did not merely *refuse* the earnest prayer), but it implicates him in another: must God be persuaded by numbers, like the mob whose numbers persuaded Pilate to deliver Jesus unto death? That seems the most blatant superstition. But most do not notice this since their attention is naturally taken up with the more obvious feelings of solidarity and mutual support inculcated when one asks others to pray on one's behalf.[143]

The Name Game

Notice that the two or three believers assembled must have gathered "in my name," a stipulation that implies they have invoked the presence of Jesus in prayer before they started. Another variable! One might easily forget to do this. Something like this stipulation appears in a string of Johannine parallels

---

143. D.Z. Phillips, *The Concept of Prayer* (London: Routledge and Kegan Paul, 1965), pp. 126–127.

to Mark 11:22–24. They include John 13:16 ("It was not you who chose [to follow] me, but I who chose you and appointed you to go forth and bear fruit, and for that fruit to remain till harvest, so that whatever you may *ask the Father in my name* he may give you."); 14:12–14, 24 ("Amen, amen: I tell you, whoever believes in me, the deeds I do, he, too, shall perform; even greater than these will he do, for I am going to the Father [and someone must do them]. And whatever you *ask in my name*, this I will do, that the Father may be glorified in the Son. If you *ask me anything in my name*, I will do it."); 16:23b-24 ("Amen, amen: I tell you, whatever you *request of the Father in my name*, he will give you. Up to now you *requested nothing in my name*; go ahead: ask, and you will receive, so that your joy may be undiluted [by any sense of lack]."). Here it has become explicit: just as James 4:2b-3a says, "You do not have for the simple reason that you do not ask! Then you ask and do not receive, because you ask wrongly." And there must be fifty ways to ask wrongly, only one to ask rightly, and who can be sure what *that* is? What exactly does it mean to pray "in Jesus' name"?

Admittedly, it might imply a blank check with Jesus' name signed to it, guaranteeing an answer. But the fact that it modifies the simple act of praying, requesting, i.e., simply in one's *own* name, subordinates prayer to Christology, imposing the creed as a presupposition for effective prayer.

Come Back Tomorrow!

Persistence is made the condition for effectual prayer in Matthew 7:7–8 ("Just ask! It shall be given you! Look for it! You will find it! Knock, and the door will swing wide for you! For every persistent asker receives, and every determined seeker finds, and for the insistent knocker it shall sooner or later be opened"). But who does not by now recognize this saying rather as a way of discounting the criticism that prayer just did not work? "I prayed and nothing happened." But did you pray *long enough*? Who told you that you can hold God to a deadline? It is like the Eight-Ball toy which pretends to answer someone's query, "Will I get a mate?" with the "answer" of "Ask again" or "The future will disclose it." It is a way of saying that an immediate, timely answer may *never* come, and you will have no right to complain. The answer, for all you may know, might have arrived the day after you gave up.

God Says No

Matthew 7:9–11 says, "Just point out a man among you who would give his son a rock if he asked him for a roll! Or, if he asked for a fish, who would give him a snake? And if you, being sinners, nonetheless know to give good gifts to your children, how much more can you expect your Father in the heavens to give good things to those who ask him?" At first this passage seems to persuade with sweet reason that one ought to expect God, as a compassionate father, to come forward with what one needs. After all, why on earth *wouldn't* he? And yet even here we detect an implication of the opposite: suppose the child, little realizing the consequences, were to ask Dad for a tasty-looking rock or a pretty snake? We must assume a good father would withhold these items rather than making his son learn his lesson the hard way, which presumably explains why God declined to grant you that relationship or that job you were praying for.

Romans 8:26–27 reads: "The Spirit, too, takes a hand in our weakness: while we do not know our own good well enough to ask for it, the Spirit itself intercedes on our behalf with inarticulate groanings; with the result that the Searcher of hearts knows the thinking of the Spirit, because he is able to ask on behalf of the saints from God's perspective." This text provides the same evasion. To wit, why do we fail to receive that for which we beseech God time and time again? Simply because God sees the big picture that we cannot see, and he knows that sometimes to grant our requests would be like the wishes granted with perverse irony in "The Monkey's Paw."

We may find that a prayer goes unanswered and never learn why (though it is usually pretty easy to come up with a few guesses), but then again we may learn that the good we had hoped to receive was in reality the enemy of the best God had for us, as Paul found out the hard way in 2 Corinthians 12:7–9 ("To prevent me from becoming swell-headed over the superabundance of revelations vouchsafed me, a thorn in the flesh was given me, an angel of the Accuser, to punish me, to prevent my self-inflation. I pleaded with the Lord three times about this, that I might become free of it. And he said to me, 'My charisma is sufficient for you, for my power is perfected in weakness'"). I'm not giving you what's behind Door Number One, Paul, because I've seen what's behind Door Number Two, and, believe me, it's a whole lot better!" Who's going to complain about that?

There is nothing at all unreasonable about this explanation. It makes plenty of sense. That is not the point. It is just that, if one were mindful of these considerations *going in*, one would scarcely have the effrontery to "claim" or "demand" things from God or even to "believe God" for this or that. We ought to envision the possibility of "No" as an answer right up front.

Prayer Warriors

As early sectarian Christianity began to settle back into conformity with worldly values and to expect less of God, those challenges once issued to all within earshot ("Sell your possessions! Leave your family and wander the roads preaching! Take up the martyr's cross! Cast out demons! Heal the sick! Speak in new tongues! It is good for a man not to touch a woman!")--they were reduced in application to a sacred elite of "hundred per centers," with everybody else let off the hook. Such is the context of 1 Corinthians chapter 13, where what were at first marks of *all* Jesus' followers have now become spiritual gifts found only among a select and celebrated few: the charismatic itinerant preachers, the celibate orders of widows and virgins, the exorcists, healers, martyrs and confessors, and prophets. Note how that in 1 Corinthians 13:1–3 mountain-moving faith has become a super-power of only such an elite, no longer expected of all believers:

> If I speak in human tongues and those of angels, but I have not love, I am merely making noise, like a trumpet blast or a crashing cymbal. If I have the mantel of prophecy and know all mysteries and all *gnosis*, and if I have complete faith so as to be able to uproot mountains at a word, but I have not love, I am nothing. And if I donate all my possessions, and if I deliver up my body to be burnt, but I have not love, I gain no heavenly reward by it.

Need I say it? This is yet another way to evade the demand for radical prayer and faith, to legitimatize tepid faith. Only Christian superheroes have faith like *that*!

Dream Catch 22

The penultimate position on the New Testament scale of prayer is occupied by 1 John 5:14: "And this is the confidence we have in him, that if we ask anything according to his will he hears us." It sounds as if we were back all at once breathing the rarified mountaintop air of Mark 11:22–24 again. But we are not. Now there is, attached like a barnacle to the hull of the promise, the proviso that only prayers which happen to accord with *what God already* had planned will be answered. Which is to say they are not answered at all, since petitioning God is moot. His will is set. If our requests happen to match it, good for us. If they don't, too bad. That sober realism we have already come to understand. But now the dilemma becomes crystal clear: *why pray at all?*

Take the case of Jesus in Gethsemane. He prays to his Father: "All things are possible for you. Let this cup pass from me; nevertheless, your will be done, not mine." Jesus lets his preference be known. But he yields to God's plan, for ultimately he shares what Immanuel Kant called "the holy will of God"— to prize one's duty above all else. But then would it not be more consistent to abbreviate the whole process, as Meister Eckhart[144] counseled? To pray nothing but "Thy will be done,"

---

144. Meister Eckhart, Sermon 17, "No respecter of persons," in *Meister Eckhart: A Modern Translation*, p. 175; "The Book of Divine Comfort," p. 49.

the goal being, not to alter God's plan (as if poor mortals might point out a better way to him!), but rather simply to align one's own will with God's infinite wisdom? Why ask anything at all?

> What is the prayer of the disinterested heart? I answer by saying that a disinterested man, pure in heart, has no prayer, for to pray is to want something from God, something added that one desires, or something that God is to take away. The disinterested person, however, wants nothing, and neither has he anything of which he would be rid. Therefore he has no prayer, or he prays only to be uniform with God.[145]

I think this is one of those places where, as Paul Tillich said, the Bible raises a philosophical question that it does not answer in philosophical terms. "If one starts to think about the meaning of biblical symbols, one is already in the midst of ontological problems."[146] Scripture raises the philosophical questions and leaves it to us to answer them. And this means that what it says about prayer finally points toward the dissolution of prayer in *pure surrender*. And this will mean that earlier New Testament passages about prayer, the ones we began with, must yield to the final insight, to be discarded, much as Shankara said all prayers, hymns, and devotions are moot once one comes to realize one's identity with the Godhead. That, in turn, is why in the Gospel of Thomas, saying 14, Jesus warns: "If you fast, you will only engender sin for yourselves. And if you pray, you will be damned. And if you give alms, you will only do your spirit harm."

---

145. Meister Eckhart, "About Disinterest," pp. 88–89.

146. Paul Tillich, *Biblical Religion and the Search for Ultimate Reality* (Chicago: University of Chicago Press, 1972), p. 83.

No More Bait and Switch

I have tried to outline the process by which the initial absolute confidence of radical prayer gave way to tepid half-belief like that of King Ahaz in Isaiah 14 who lacked the spine to name a sign for Jehovah to perform for him. One proviso, one condition, one bit of fine print after another finally whittled away that radical faith until in the end all such faith, assuming as it did a privileged knowledge of the secret will of God that no mortal possesses, dissolved into surrender. Seen this way, petitionary prayer turns out to be a cocoon from which a kind of Taoist passivity emerges like a butterfly. It would mean petitionary prayer is a childish thing to be transcended by the mature.

But is it? It is too easy to sacrifice familiar religious experiences to the unfeeling logic of systematic theology. Should we cut loose biblical personalism, the notion, at bottom, that there is somehow Someone listening to us? Think of the Three Young Men in the fiery furnace. "Our God, whom we serve, is able to deliver us from the burning fiery furnace; and he will deliver us out of your clutches, O king. But if not, know this, O king: we will not serve your gods or bow before the golden image you erected" (Dan. 3:17–18). They pray in confidence that God can do anything he pleases, including answering one's specific prayer. But being a puny mortal, one does not presume to know God's will in every situation. He may have his own reasons for not answering, and that is his business. The attitude of Shadrach, Meshach, and Abed-Nego was *confidence without presumption*. It is the sheer faith that God can do anything, together with the Socratic humility to admit one cannot know what God will choose to do. That humility is not doubt. It is only to recognize the freedom of God to do anything, to act "outside the box" in which we seek to trap him when we dictate alternatives to him in our prayers.

D.Z. Phillips makes much of this, seeking to reveal the "depth grammar" of Christian prayer language. He admits that, according to the "surface grammar," petitionary prayer is superstitious, as if mere mortals could tell God his business and succeed in altering physical events. But not so fast! Look just below this surface level and you will see something that deserves respect. He notes that pious suppliants always either explicitly or implicitly suffix their requests with "Thy will be done." In other words, they are humbly (one might say *realistically*) acknowledging that it is up to God; he will do as he sees fit, and the one praying is perfectly willing to acquiesce to the outcome. After all, the believer is making a request, not a demand. Granted, as we have seen, there are inflated promises in the New Testament that must encourage superstitious overconfidence in prayer, overconfidence that pushes the suppliant over the line into magic, making God into a genie. I will take that up in what follows. But for the present I simply want to emphasize that prayer is not necessarily or essentially superstition. Phillips[147] speaks of religious devotion in terms very similar to those of Schleiermacher (who, strangely does not come in for mention in Phillips's book, a fact which makes the parallel all the more striking). Both regard genuine piety as essentially a stance of dependence upon God, a God understood as transcending mythological personalism. Schleiermacher called it "the feeling [i.e., sense or awareness] of absolute dependence."[148]

---

147. Phillips, *Concept of Prayer*, Chapter 5, "Prayer and Dependence," pp. 81–111.

148. Friedrich Schleiermacher, *The Christian Faith*. Volume 1.

The error of prayer we have seen to be a misplaced confidence, not in the power of God, but in our ability to know what he would want to do. One thing is safe to say we know, though: if we reduce God to a genie beholden to our whims, we have created an idol who will never hear our prayers or anything else. But then there is another important question to be raised at this very point. Does the very notion of a deity who hears prayers and answers them itself imply that God is an idol? Schleiermacher suggests that

> prayer seems really to be heard only when because of it an event happens which would not otherwise have happened: thus there seems to be the suspension of an effect which, according to the interrelatedness of nature, should have followed. . . . [But] prayer and its fulfillment are only part of the original divine plan, and consequently the idea that otherwise something else might have happened is wholly meaningless.[149]

Tillich warns that "If prayer] is brought down to the level of a conversation between two beings, it is blasphemous and ridiculous. If, however, it is understood as the 'elevation of the heart,' namely, the center of the personality, to God, it is a revelatory event."[150]

Phillips writes very similarly:

Trans. D.M. Baillie, W.R. Matthews, Edith Sandbach-Marshall, A.B. Macaulay, Alexander Grieve, J.Y. Campbell, R.W. Stewart, and H.R. Mackintosh. Harper Torchbooks (NY: Harper & Row, 1963), pp. 12–15, etc.

149. Schleiermacher, *Christian Faith*. Volume 1, p. 180.

150. Tillich, *Systematic Theology*, p. 127.

The analogy between talking to a person and talking to God is strictly limited. [Otherwise the notion of] talking to God would be to make God a language-user, someone who comes to know what he did not know previously, someone who has to learn what things mean, and one from whom secrets can be kept. In other words, to fail to limit the analogy is to cease to talk of the God whom people worship as the all-knowing God from whom no secrets are hid, meaning by this not One to whom in fact all secrets are told, but rather, One from whom it is logically impossible to hide anything.[151]

These statements, taken together, mean that a properly exalted God-concept makes "God" not so much "the Supreme Being" as "Being-itself," the "Ground of Being." God, then, is not a link in the causal chain operative in "creation," i.e., the world we live in. "He" permeates all things (or underlies all things) but is not *one of* the things, not even the Supreme Thing. God is not a beneficent person, no cosmic Santa Claus, no Aladdin's Genie, even if our requests of "him" are entirely unselfish and philanthropic. Again, God is not an operator on the other end of a Dial-A-Prayer line. It might be better to compare him to the phone line itself. Both Schleiermacher and Tillich come close to Pantheism,[152] but Schleiermacher implicitly goes as far as Monism. When he says that a mortal's prayer and its reply are both part of a preordained system, is he not implying that we are praying to a subordinated god, like the Vedantic Isvara

---

151. Phillips, *Concept of Prayer*, p. 113.

152. See Julia A. Lamm, *The Living God: Schleiermacher's Theological Appropriation of Spinoza* (University Park: Pennsylvania State University Press, 1996), Chapter 4, "Limits and Method: The Coincidence of Divine Causality and the Nature-System," pp. 127–157.

or the Gnostic Demiurge? By contrast God Proper lies outside this sandbox, this ant farm of *maya, Samsara*.

The personal God is the mythological God. Bultmann explains that the objectification of God leads straight to mythology.

> Mythology expresses a certain understanding of human existence. It believes that the world and human life have their ground and their limits in a power which is beyond all that we can calculate or control. Mythology speaks about this power inadequately and insufficiently because it speaks about it as if it were a worldly power. It speaks of gods who represent the power beyond the visible, comprehensible world. It speaks of gods as if they were men and of their actions as human actions, although it conceives of the gods as endowed with superhuman power and of their actions as incalculable, as capable of breaking the normal, ordinary order of events. It may be said that myths give to the transcendent reality an immanent, this-worldly objectivity. Myths give worldly objectivity to that which is unworldly.[153]

> As for the Christian theology, can you imagine anything more appallingly idiotic than the Christian idea of heaven? What kind of deity is it that would be capable of creating angels and men to sing his praises day and night to all eternity? It is, of course, the figure of the Oriental despot, with his inane and barbaric vanity. Such a conception is an insult to God. (Alfred North Whitehead)[154]

---

153. Rudolf Bultmann, *Jesus Christ and Mythology* (NY: Scribners, 1958), p. 19.

154. Lucien Price, *Dialogues of Alfred North Whitehead* (Boston: Little, Brown and Company, 1954), p. 277.

"What surprises me is that so many Christian philosophers seem to be talking about a natural, as opposed to a supernatural, God; a God who is an existent among existents, and an agent among agents."[155] By a "natural God" Phillips appears to mean what Pascal called the God of Abraham, Isaac, and Jacob, the God of biblical personalism, as opposed to a "supernatural God," Pascal's God of the Philosophers. The latter is an entity beyond definition, since *definition* implies *finitude*. Such a God is Being-itself, exalted above any subject-object distinction, not a being, not even the supreme being. Tillich reiterates:

> [Myth] uses material from our ordinary experience. It puts the stories of the gods into the framework of time and space although it belongs to the nature of the ultimate to be beyond time and space. . . . Even [the] one God is an object of mythological language, and if spoken about is drawn into the framework of time and space.[156]

This radical enlargement of the God-concept carries wide-ranging implications for prayer. For one thing, it is no longer clear that God is a hearer, much less an answerer, of prayers. A dialogue partner? Unlikely. "In short, all the stories in which divine-human interactions are told are [to be] considered mythological in character, and objects of demythologization."[157] For another, can we imagine such an entity interfering with or intervening in worldly affairs? Mustn't "he" transcend the chain of cause and effect? If God is truly beyond the categories

---

155. Phillips, *Concept of Prayer*, p. 83.

156. Tillich, *Dynamics of Faith*, p. 49.

157. Tillich, *Dynamics of Faith*, p. 50.

of space and time, it could make no sense to posit God as *doing* much of anything. Friedrich Schleiermacher saw this.

> we must . . . try, as far as possible, to interpret every event with reference to the interdependence of nature and without detriment to that principle. Now some have represented miracles in this sense as essential to the perfect manifestation of the divine omnipotence. But it is difficult to conceive, on the one side, how omnipotence is shown to be greater in the suspension of the interdependence of nature than in its original immutable course which was no less divinely ordered. For, indeed, the capacity to make a change in what has been ordained is only a merit in the ordainer, if a change is necessary, which again can only be the result of some imperfection in him or in his work. If such interference be postulated as one of the privileges of the Supreme Being, it would first have to be assumed that there is something not ordained by Him which could offer him resistance.[158]

Phillips has pretty much the same idea.

> The concept of divine power is a difficult one. Power usually implies resistance. Power is that which enables one to overcome resistance. But this cannot be applied to belief in God as an omnipotent Creator. What could resistance to the Creator be? The difficulty is in speaking of God as having to overcome resistance; a difficulty that arises because one tries to press the analogy between human power and divine power; an analogy which . . . at best only leads to idolatry.[159]

---

158. Schleiermacher, *Christian Faith*, p. 179.

159. Phillips, *Concept of Prayer*, p. 128.

Miracles cannot be interpreted in terms of a supranatural interference in natural processes. If such an interpretation were true, the manifestation of the ground of being would destroy the structure of being ... A genuine miracle is first of all an event which is astonishing, unusual, shaking, without contradicting the rational structure of reality" (Paul Tillich).[160]

All this raises a kindred question that is too often ignored, both by believers and disbelievers in the supernatural. What *is* the "supernatural"? What is the meaning of the term? It may turn out to be a synonym for, you guessed it: superstition.

The Ionian pre-Socratic thinker Thales is considered the father of both science and philosophy, no mean feat! Thales was willing to allow that Zeus made the rain to fall, as mythology dictated. But he went on to ask the crucial question: *How* does Zeus do it? There must be some *way* that he does it, right? And if you agree to that much, you are saying that God/Zeus is a discrete being who employs/manipulates laws of nature as yet unknown to lesser beings, namely you and me. This sounds like Erich von Däniken's theory that the gods of mythology were actually space aliens who worked their legendary wonders by means of super-science. Think of the hilarious scene in *Star Trek IV: The Voyage Home* in which Captain Kirk and Doctor McCoy are trying to rescue a seriously injured Commander Chekov from the dangers of primitive twentieth-century medicine. McCoy: "We're dealing with medievalism here, Jim!" On his way out, McCoy sees an old woman about to undergo dialysis and gives her a pill that instantly grows a new kidney. A miracle? No, just medicine far in advance

---

160. Tillich, *Systematic Theology*, pp. 116, 117.

of our own. Members of Flying Saucer cults understand the miracles of Jesus precisely in these terms. This is of a piece with eighteenth-century Protestant Rationalism—you know, the idea that Jesus didn't really walk on the water but just knew where the stepping stones were. But if you are a traditionalist Christian who believes Jesus did walk on the surface of the Sea of Galilee, *how do you think he did it?* Even assuming he was the Son of God, even God incarnate, there must be *some way that he did it.* Otherwise, we're talking about cartoons.[161] Or magic, and that's superstition.

Mystery, Miracle, and Authority

I don't think religion is merely a device for social control. At least not all of it, not all the time. Religion haters like to oversimplify the matter so they can criticize it more easily. But even the significant element of truth in the caricature is only half the picture, because the other half is that people are ever eager to be led, to be dominated. They feel they cannot bear the responsibility to think and to decide for themselves. This is the sobering insight set forth in Dostoevsky's *The Brothers Karamazov*, in Ivan Karamazov's prose poem of the Grand Inquisitor.

The scene is Seville in Spain in the darkest days of the Spanish Inquisition. Nightly the air is lit with the upright pyres of heretics condemned for daring to think for themselves,

---

161. "This argument confuses Walt Disney with metaphysics." Leonard Piekoff, "The Analytic-Synthetic Dichotomy" in Ayn Rand, ed., *Introduction to Objectivist Epistemology* (NY: Objectivist, 1969), p. 156. Thanks to my friend Russ Farrington for tracking this quote down for me!

having the effrontery to challenge the authority of God's self-appointed vicars and to decide for themselves what is the truth. With unerring instinct it is here that Jesus Christ chooses to return to earth, not as a conquering lion, but once again as an unassuming lamb. The humble of the land once again flock to him, and he heals their sick. As he once did in the village of Nain, he halts a funeral procession on its way into a church and takes the hand of the young girl, saying to her, *Talitha cumi*, little maid, arise! However, the hosannas of the crowd do little to warm the heart of the Grand Inquisitor who happens to be present. He has seen enough, and Jesus is arrested on the spot. After all, wasn't he, and doesn't he remain, the greatest of heretics?

The next day the cardinal pays his ostensible Lord a call in jail and proceeds to catechize him in the religious wisdom of the world. In short he tells Jesus that in fostering a kind of spiritual aristocracy for those few who would dare to think for themselves, Jesus was laying a burden on mankind that it just could not bear. It has been the great work of the Church in all the centuries since then to lift that burden and to provide the security of authoritarianism, of unthinking obedience, to hold in trust for the common person the gift of his soul. Thus the Church lifts the terrible burden of freedom, a burden bearable only by a spiritual Atlas like Jesus.

Why is Jesus in jail? Simply because the Church cannot allow him to gum up the works again! He must be stopped before he can again, like some sort of spiritual terrorist, release the infection of freedom and autonomy to plague the sheeplike flock of humanity. Once he went to the cross, now he will go to the stake, and not a moment too soon!

There is an unholy trinity of factors on which the Inquisitor's plan hinges. They are *miracle*, *mystery*, and *authority*. What is their interconnection? It is fairly simple: *Miracle* subverts the rational order of nature and leaves the jaw slack with wonder. Miracle compels belief in the power that was able to conjure it. "Who then is this, that wind and sea obey him!" Prodigies force belief, driving rational argument from the field.

A contrast between Mark and Matthew is instructive here. In both, the crowds exclaim, "A new teaching, and with authority!" But what prompts this exclamation? In Matthew it is the hearing of the Sermon on the Mount, but in Mark it is the spectacle of Jesus exorcising a demon. Do you see the difference? In one gospel, it is the inherent power of the teaching that wins his hearers' hearts, but in the other, they are simply bowled over by a magic trick, and hence whatever he says must be true!

Mystery is the charmed circle where arbitrary beliefs hide behind a false screen of holiness, like the all-too-human Wizard of Oz behind his curtain, hoping you will pay no attention to the artifice. There are genuine mysteries, realities too great or too subtle for the mind to plumb. But the Inquisitor and his brethren call mystery that which is indeed amenable to rational scrutiny but which would not for many moments survive it. The accursed multitude cannot be allowed to consider for themselves, else they might come to some conclusion the Church deems dangerous to their souls.

The relationship between miracle and mystery was perfectly set forth by Lessing. He discounted the traditional proof from miracle by asking us to imagine a mystagogue who proposes to "prove" that "2+2=3" by making a ball vanish into thin air. Suppose he *does* actually make the ball vanish! Do two and two suddenly equal three? No, of course they do not. The miracle only proves the miracle can be done, nothing more. But if you think it *does* prove 2+2=3, you have allowed miracle to whisk you away into the zone of credulity where reason abdicates its seat and any absurdity may be believed, as long as it is dignified by the rubric "mystery."

And who is it that makes balls to disappear and catechizes that 2+2=3? Who chooses what absurdities to dress up as mysteries? Well, who was it in Orwell's *1984* who had poor Winston Smith believing that 2+2=3 before it was over? It was Big Brother. It was the Grand Inquisitor. It was Authority.

Authority here is a particular *kind* of authority. It is arrogated authority, authority *usurped*. It is, remember, not the authority that truth commands by the nobility of its own manifest virtue, but rather that commandeered by the bribery, the cajoling, the compulsion of miracle. It is the kind of authority that rests upon mysteries which are but mystifications, the cheat authority of the man behind the curtain. Yet at the same time, it is not an authority imposed on the conscience by anyone but the owner of the conscience. It is authority given freely to the one who promises to trade peace for freedom.

The Grand Inquisitor and his religion are like the great systems of political authoritarianism. Did Hitler and Mussolini *seize* power? Or weren't they *given* power by populations who were tired of the inefficiency and the dangers of freedom? And don't huge churches fill up again and again because their members cannot dispense with the burden of freedom fast enough? They will yield it to any charismatic demagogue who promises them the security of inerrant dogmas and a ticket to an imaginary heaven of true believers as a reward for unquestioning assent.

The Inquisitor's religion is like a security alarm service for the mind. It promises "perfect peace" as long as you are hooked into the system. You just embrace the prescribed dogmas, and any time an unorthodox thought dares approach your mental fortress, the alarm begins to sound. "Heresy!" "False Doctrine!" Warning! Alert!

Conclusion: Superstitionatural

I hope to have shown that the source of superstition in Christianity is the objectification of the transcendent. It is the drawing down of that which words cannot express into a system of words and ideas derived from finite, mundane existence. As the Taoist epigram puts it, "Those who know don't say; those who say don't know." They don't say because they know they *can't* say. As for those who do say, what they don't know is that their words are not conveying the truth but *obscuring* it, even *substituting* for it. And that is idolatry. Or, to apply another cliché, the God of the Patriarchs should have yielded, like the Old Year to the New, to the God of the Philosophers. But he didn't. Christianity continues to pour the new wine into old, superannuated skins. Of, if you prefer another slogan, "Christianity is our Old Testament."[162]

Let's review some of the superstitions of Christianity to remind ourselves how they all stem from the mythological

162. Don Cupitt, *Taking Leave of God* (NY: Crossroad Publishing, 1981), p. 146.

version of God. The much-vaunted notion of Jesus as one's personal savior, a two thousand year old individual in the sky (or some other dimension?) somehow able to carry on devotional conversations with (or at least to listen to) millions of devotees at the same time. It amounts to childish gibberish because of its impossible juxtaposition of *infinity* and *individuality*. This Jesus is the holy oxymoron Francis A. Schaffer used to call "the Infinite-Personal God," something that can't even be false, let alone true, as it is just a string of words. And this raises the Christological irony. Just as Jesus the imaginary friend is a figment of subjective faith, so the Christ of the Creeds is manifestly a cumulative contrivance of religious theoreticians hammering out a metaphysical chimera possessing this and that attribute needed to satisfy one's preferred formula. And the greatest irony is that the same theologians insisted that they were doing nothing more than marking the boundaries of the Mystery that cannot be explained, even though they had just explained the daylights out of it! It's like pretending to map out terra incognita.

What has happened here can best be understood according to the insights of a couple of scholars. First, Rudolf Otto, who describes the pre-rational *numinous* experience of the Holy, the Wholly Other. Both theology and mythology are attempts in various ways to make some kind of sense of the experience, in other words, to *rationalize* it, perhaps in hopes of providing a trigger for more people to have the experience. But inevitably the myths and doctrines take the place of the experience. The other scholar I have in mind is psychologist Abraham Maslow.[163] He explains this subsequent process of

163. Abraham H. Maslow, *Religions, Values, and Peak-Experiences* (NY: Viking Press, 1970), pp. 21–25.

ossification in terms of the personality types of the "peaker," the one who has the initial encounter (usually unsought) with the Numinous, and the non-peaker who tries to translate the founder's pre-rational experience of revelation into a doctrine and a ritual. Jesus, according to Maslow, would be the peaker, Paul the theoretician. Joseph Smith would be the peaker, Brigham Young the administrator.

I suggest that the Holy, without name or story, corresponds to the *Nirguna Brahman* ("Brahman without qualities"), *Sunyata* ("the Void," "Suchness"), the Cloud of Unknowing, the God beyond God, the Desert of the Godhead.[164] As soon as theologians theologize it they objectify it, mythologize it. And God becomes a being among beings. His miracles, I have argued, must be manipulations of higher laws unknown to primitive mortals. He listens to worshippers, takes their advice and changes his plans, grants their requests like a department store Santa Claus.

Otto speaks of the *Mysterium Tremendum*, the holy terror that seizes the one who encounters the Wholly Other. It is overwhelming awe before which we shrink into awareness of our ontological insignificance. This is the proper meaning of "the fear of the Lord." It has become degraded into mythical primitivism when we feel we must cringe in fear of God's smiting fist at the slightest hint of disobedience.

We are beginning to glimpse the outlines of a non-mythical, non-theological, non-superstitious Christianity. It would abandon the demand that Christians sign on the dotted lines of incomprehensible creeds. It would make no prayer requests since no one is listening to us, but *we* would do the listening,

---

164. Meister Eckhart, Sermon 22, "God hinders the best," pp. 200–201.

as we contemplate the fact of the inarticulable Greatness. We would rejoice in the charming and edifying stories of scripture, the poetry of liturgy, singing the creed[165] rather than believing it as we believe that $E=mc^2$. As for Jesus, we would no longer anxiously define him but rather encounter him as a great literary figure and make him our fictively personified conscience as Zinzendorf and the old Pietists did. Face it: that's all you're really doing anyway. And it's enough.

Amazingly, to leave behind the personal, i.e., objectified, mythological deity of Christian tradition in favor of the God of Spinoza, Shankara, Tillich, and Bultmann, the Holy Without Qualities, would seem even to render moot the supposed difference between theism and atheism![166] As Tillich said, the God rejected by the atheists indeed does not exist.[167] There is no watchful Jehovah observing the deeds of men from a throne above the blue sky. One cannot properly say that "God" (Being-itself) "exists," since "existence" applies to an existing thing. To "ex-ist" denotes protruding as an individual from the Ground of Being, from existence itself. God is beyond "existence." I should think that with this insight the whole question has changed. It becomes more of a question of whether one embraces philosophical Idealism. The question is that of whether and in what sense Truth, Love, the Holy, the Infinite, etc., are "real." Schleiermacher was careful to define

---

165. James A. Pike used to say he couldn't bring himself to *say* the creed but *could* sing it.

166. Tillich, *Dynamics of Faith*, pp. 46–47: "It is obvious that such an understanding of the meaning of God makes the discussions about the existence or non-existence of God meaningless . . .. If 'existence' refers to something that can be found within the whole of reality, no divine being exists."

167. Tillich, *Systematic Theology,* p. 205, 245.

piety as "a sense and taste for the Infinite." That's not theism. That's not Jehovah.

About the Author

Robert M. Price is a freethought advocate who has written on many subjects in many venues, and for many years. He has been at various times an agnostic, an exponent of Liberal Protestant theology, a non-theist, a secular humanist, a religious humanist, a Unitarian-Universalist wannabe, an unaffiliated Universalist, and a Fellow of the Jesus Seminar. Any way you cut it, his name is Legion. Not your typical atheist, Price continues to love the various great religions as endlessly fascinating creations/expressions of the human spirit. He loves theology, too. He hosts The Bible Geek and The Human Bible podcasts, and indeed the Bible is his main focus of interest. He is the author of numerous books, including *Beyond Born Again*, *Deconstructing Jesus*, and *Inerrant the Wind*. He is the founder and editor of the *Journal of Higher Criticism* and has debated William Lane Craig, Bart Ehrman, Craig Blomberg, and others. He lives in North Carolina.